DETROIT AND THE PROBLEM OF ORDER, 1830–1880

DETROIT
AND THE
PROBLEM
OF ORDER,
1830–1880

A Geography of
Crime, Riot, and Policing

John C. Schneider

University of Nebraska Press
Lincoln and London

Copyright © 1980 by the
University of Nebraska Press
All rights reserved

Library of Congress Cataloging in Publication Data

Schneider, John C 1945–
   Detroit and the problem of order, 1830–1880.

   Includes bibliographical references and index.
   1. Detroit—Police—History—19th century.   2. Urbanization—Michigan—Detroit—History—19th   century.   3. Crime   and   criminals—Michigan—Detroit—
History—19th century.   I.   Title.
HV 8148.D452S36   363.2'09774'34   79–16492
ISBN 0–8032–4113–5

Manufactured in the United States of America

For
Suzanne,
Olivia,
and David

CONTENTS

TABLES

MAPS

ACKNOWLEDGMENTS

I began research for this book in 1975 during a leave of absence from my teaching responsibilities, and for that I am indebted to the Advisory Committee (1974–75) of the History Department at the University of Nebraska–Lincoln. A summer fellowship from the university's Research Council made it possible for me to devote additional time exclusively to the project. The Research Council also provided a grant-in-aid to cover the costs of the several maps prepared for this study. Kenneth Engelbrecht and John Giardino, both graduate assistants in the Geography Department at the University of Nebraska–Lincoln during 1976–77, were the able cartographers.

The staff of the Burton Historical Collection at the Detroit Public Library assisted me courteously and efficiently during the many months I was there pestering it for this or that. I want to thank particularly the Curator of the Burton Collection, Joseph Oldenburg, from whose knowledge of the Detroit City Archives I benefited considerably. The staffs of the various libraries of the University of Michigan, Ann Arbor, were most helpful, as were the staffs of the Michigan Historical Collections, Ann Arbor, the Michigan State Library, Lansing, and the Michigan State Archives, Lansing.

Some of the material in this study appeared earlier in different form in the *Journal of Urban History, Michigan History,* and *Detroit in Perspective: A Journal of Regional History.* Patrice Berger and Eric Monkkonen each read carefully a first draft of the book itself and made many valuable suggestions. Others who offered encouragement or constructive criticism along the way were JoEllen Vinyard, Mark Haller, Bryan Thompson, Roger Lane, Harold Pepinsky, Eugene Watts, Michael Isenberg, and Benjamin Rader. My colleague Frederick Luebke has helped and inspired me in more ways than he could ever imagine.

My wife's parents, Ray and Mae Spencer, now living in Marquette, Michigan, graciously relinquished the basement of their house in Ypsilanti while I conducted research in Detroit and Ann Arbor for the better part of 1975. Suzanne and our children, Olivia and David, put up with me throughout all of this, and for that I am most grateful of all.

Detroit and the Problem of Order, 1830–1880

INTRODUCTION

The nineteenth century transformed the American city. In 1830 it was a relatively compact place. People could walk without too much difficulty from one end to the other, and in fact almost all of them went about their daily tasks entirely on foot. The sense of a shared "community" may not have existed, but at least a comprehensibility, even an intimacy, prevailed. By 1880, however, the old walking city had given way to urban sprawl. Streets seemed to stretch to the horizon, and the city engulfed what had not long before been open field and empty space. To get around, many people now used the horse-drawn trolleys that glided along the principal avenues. Some urbanites were no longer sure what the other side of town looked like.

No less sweeping an alteration took place in the way urban space was organized. We know now that as early as the 1760s American cities began to develop recognizable sub-areas based on the occupations of the residents or on the nature of the work done there. Still, the urban environment in the early nineteenth century was characterized by only minimal specialized land use. Dwellings, shops, and stores of all kinds mixed together in many parts of the city. Some urbanites had to endure the odor of putrefying animal wastes wafting through their windows from slaughterhouses next door. By the late nineteenth century, on the other hand, the city's spatial arrangements showed more differentiation. The central business district, secondary business strips along the streetcar lines, factory and warehouse districts, fashionable residential streets, working-class neighborhoods, poverty-rid-

1

den and blighted slums, even clearly delineated vice quarters —all made up the city that was well on its way to becoming the environment early twentieth-century sociologists would define as a segmented ecosystem.

The city's physical layout is not a mere stage on which urbanites act out interests operating independently of it. The spatial surroundings in which urbanites find themselves have a great deal to do with the way they think and act, as individuals or as groups. David Harvey, a geographer who has made one of the more determined efforts to explore the relationship between urban space and social behavior, writes that "once a particular spatial form is created it tends to institutionalize and, in some respects, to determine the future development of the social process." Since spatial form and social process are complementary, engaged in a constantly interacting dynamic, he contends that one cannot be understood without the other, and they should be separated for analytical but not theoretical purposes.[1]

Sensitivity to the spatial variable in social behavior is quite appropriate to historical analysis, certainly in the study of the rapidly growing and changing nineteenth-century American city. John T. Cumbler argues that the locational patterns of work and residence go a long way toward explaining historical varieties in urban working-class behavior. If the shoemakers of Lynn, Massachusetts, he says, showed more class consciousness and solidarity after the middle of the nineteenth century than did the textile workers of Fall River, it was because their work places, residences, and entertainment areas all remained centrally located, while those of the textile workers did not. This contiguity integrated a variety of work and social activities, generating more cohesion among the workers and facilitating the assimilation of new members into the work force.[2]

Historians could proceed just as profitably with a spatial approach to the study of law and order—crime, mob violence, and policing—in the nineteenth-century city. To date, scholars have for the most part treated the space and form of the city as a backdrop, a setting in which criminals acted, mobs rioted, and policemen patrolled, but which remained a passive force in these strictly social, economic, or political matters. Sam Bass

Warner, Jr., is one of the few historians who have tried to understand the meaning of urban spatial development for the problem of public order in the nineteenth century. In his provocative study of Philadelphia, Warner argues that the frenetic and unregulated physical growth of the emerging "big city" in 1830–60 tore apart the fabric of traditional neighborhood life necessary to maintain order against the stresses of rapid change, particularly new ethnic and racial heterogeneity. With a variety of self-conscious groups exposed to one another in a compact, amorphous city, street disorders became rampant. As the city expanded in the late nineteenth century, however, and as income began to replace occupation and ethnicity as the basis for residential clustering, potentially hostile groups rubbed collective shoulders less often, and neighborhood disorder all but disappeared.[3] Warner's is a good argument. Yet Bruce Laurie, studying the same Philadelphia in the 1840s, finds that whatever the impact on neighborhood life in these years, there were still some residents, particularly young men, whose attachment to their neighborhoods helped generate the competition among local gangs and fire companies that contributed to much of the city's day-to-day street violence. What really was the nature of neighborhood feelings, then, and did they or did they not encourage disorder? The matter seems worth pursuing.[4]

The study of nineteenth-century Detroit that follows integrates analyses of crime, mob violence, and police development with an analysis of the city's spatial evolution. It offers a view of the law-and-order problem as it was rooted in what more than anything else made Detroit a city: the arrangement of many people and activities in a compact setting. Why Detroit? It was a community in the mainstream of American urbanization. Growing in population from two thousand to one-hundred-sixteen thousand between 1830 and 1880, it typified the growth of the American city; but ranking as only the nation's twenty-third largest in 1850 and seventeenth largest in 1870, it was not so big as to be more representative of the urban giants whose experiences may have been unique.

Detroit's spatial arrangements operated on the history of the city's law and order in two ways. First, they were the medium through which social and economic developments were given concrete meaning. The extent to which urbanites understand their world as a series of spatial relationships rather than strictly social or economic ones is a subject that scholars from various disciplines have pursued with considerable energy. Kevin Lynch, a city planner, and Peter Gould and Rodney White, both geographers, have described how urbanites establish an image or a "mental topography" of their city, in which certain areas and their distinguishing features show up in different ways, depending on the spatial and structural drama of the area itself, or on the residence and character of the person drawing the mental image. Gerald Suttles, a sociologist, adds that urbanites translate their perceptions of the city into an arrangement of neighborhood "turfs," which they use to establish their own identity, and everyone else's, and to serve as guidelines for a variety of actions and decisions, not the least of which are political.[5]

In his elegant study of Springfield, Massachusetts, Michael Frisch demonstrates the usefulness of some of these ideas for historical analysis, especially study of the town-into-city process that overwhelmed so many communities in the nineteenth century. Frisch concentrates on the perceptions of urban change and administrative needs held by Springfield's elite residents, whose influence over the larger decision-making process was considerable. Springfield's expanding and changing physical layout was a principal ingredient in the making of an "idea of community" among influential citizens, at the same time that it became the vehicle by means of which these same residents could see expressed in architectural form their vision of city progress.[6] In Detroit, as in other nineteenth-century cities, men of property and standing were in the forefront of the police reform movement. It was one of the ways in which powerful urbanites sought to fill the essential needs of a growing and changing community, which they knew and understood from a certain spatial perspective, not just a socioeconomic one.

The second link between Detroit's geography and the history of its law and order was more direct. Spatial arrangements made for settings in which crime and disorder were more or less likely to occur. That mob violence in mid-nineteenth-century American cities, Detroit among them, was predominantly intergroup violence reveals how tense and difficult relations were among the residents of extraordinarily heterogeneous communities. There had to be settings that brought potentially hostile groups together in a provocative manner, and in which group tensions could become violent. In the same way for crime, there had to be settings that enhanced the opportunities but not the risks for the criminally disposed. Many crimes are spontaneous—family violence and drunken assaults, for example. Many others are premeditated, or at least opportunistic, and for these crimes the proper environment is critical. A dark and infrequently traveled street would be one such environment. Another would be the regular presence of criminally inclined and vulnerable persons in the same neighborhood, such as a skid row. In the dynamic young city of Detroit during the period from 1830 to 1880, the constantly changing environment, with the addition of new areas and the transformation of old ones, had a profound impact on the levels of crime and disorder.

The problem of law and order in Detroit, then, was as much as anything a problem in urban geography. The city's outward expansion, coupled with the development of a pattern of differentiated land use, operated in critical ways on Detroit's crime, mob violence, and policing. The geography of the city helped to determine where criminals acted and mobs rioted, who was victimized by criminals and rioters, and why formal police procedures took on greater importance for some people and not others.

ONE

Trouble in the Neighborhoods

On a chilly December night in 1849, a crowd of at least sixty persons, armed with crowbars, quietly and carefully tore up fifty rods of Detroit & Pontiac Railroad track running along Gratiot Street on the near northeast side of Detroit. The leaders of this little mob were no ruffians from a disreputable underclass. They included Stephen Morse, who had a butcher shop and the year before had been an alderman on the Common Council; C. G. Solyer, a grocer who was then serving as a ward constable; John V. Ruehle and William Paton, both grocers; and John Sutherland, coffinmaker. These men found themselves out on the street together tearing up track that December night because they all had shops on Gratiot Street and were not happy about the noisy locomotives rumbling past their front doors, spewing hot ashes and clouds of thick smoke. More than a year earlier, Alderman Morse had presented to his colleagues on the Common Council a petition from Ruehle and "260 others" that branded the tracks a public nuisance and called for their forcible removal. The aldermen at that point gave the railroad six months to move the tracks. The six months went by and the tracks remained. In the spring of 1849, the council recommended that the city attorney explore legal maneuvers to remedy the problem. This led to a suit, but the case moved too slowly through the judicial process for those opposed to the tracks, and their impatience finally made them reach for their crowbars. Even then, the matter was not settled. The railroad relaid the tracks in February 1850, only to

7

see them torn up again by another mob. When the Common Council agreed in July to let the railroad run its cars, for the time being at least, along Gratiot Street, residents and shop-keepers met to voice their objections, arguing that the tracks constituted a safety hazard, undermined property values, and lowered the quality of life in the area. It was not until 1852 that the Detroit & Pontiac moved its station to the riverfront and re-routed its engines along Dequindre Street, in a still largely unpopulated area on the city's outer east side.[1]

The neighborhood sensitivity and pugnacity exhibited in this affair were not uncommon in Detroit as it grew to urban maturity at mid-century, nor was the violence that stemmed from it. An increasingly heterogeneous population was find-ing its way to the city, searching for living space in the midst of an assortment of urban activities. The competition for space took place quietly, a day-to-day process of considerable impor-tance to the people and interests involved, but one visible to the observer primarily in the shape and form of the city it was creating. Yet occasionally the competition turned from process to event, leaving more palpable evidence of its development. Such was the case in Detroit during the 1850s, when the resolution of at least one part of the struggle for urban turf fell time and again into the hands of the street mob.

EARLY GROWTH AND PUBLIC ORDER

Detroit was an old community. Founded by the French in 1701 and passing to the English in 1763 and then to the Americans in 1796, it remained no more than a fort and trading village on an isolated frontier. Even with the great western migration in the years after 1815, Michigan Territory was bypassed in favor of the Ohio Valley to the south. The soil was supposedly unproductive, the climate unhealthy. Nonetheless, settlers trickled into the territory by the 1820s, and with the comple-tion of the Erie Canal in New York, the construction of roads in northern Ohio, and the federal government's efforts to im-prove Lake Erie harbors, the trickle grew to a flood in the 1830s.[2]

The peopling of Michigan brought Detroit a new prosperity as it became a point of entry for travelers heading into the interior. A town of barely thirteen hundred souls in 1824, Detroit was a booming city of seven thousand by 1836. Although the panic of 1837 and the decline in land speculation hurt Detroit and slowed its growth, the population continued to climb, reaching thirteen thousand in 1845. By then the city was a commercial center. One of every three steamers plying the waters of Lake Erie was registered at Detroit. Several railroads stretched out from the city into the countryside. Michigan grain went east by way of Detroit as early as the 1830s, while the city's wholesale-retail trade expanded rapidly.[3]

Detroit was to have grown with a baroque plan drawn up in the aftermath of a disastrous fire in 1805 by a territorial official who admired L'Enfant's Washington, D.C. Whatever the merits of this "cobweb" plan, it was considered by most Detroiters to be the product of a "wild and eccentric mind," and it was quickly mutilated. By the 1830s, the city had settled into the classic grid pattern, and only fragments of the old plan remained as a curious monument to one man's ideal (Map I–1). The grid was more suited to the growth of the 1830s, when expediency and speculation governed the city's expansion, and when entrepreneurs turned every building they could find into a hotel, a boarding house, or a general store for the outfitting of settlers.[4]

Amid the confusion, a small measure of order emerged in the city's spatial patterns. The principal commercial district, mostly dry goods stores and retail and wholesale groceries, was on Jefferson Avenue between Griswold and Randolph streets and on Woodward Avenue from Jefferson to the river. On Griswold above Jefferson and on Jefferson east of Randolph, there were the beginnings of residential enclaves of merchants, lawyers, and "gentlemen." On a few streets, particularly Franklin and Larned on the east side, none but the working class made its home. This was generally true of the city's small alleyways as well. Still, Detroit in the 1830s was not a city whose land use was highly differentiated. Stores and workshops mixed with residences in almost every corner of the

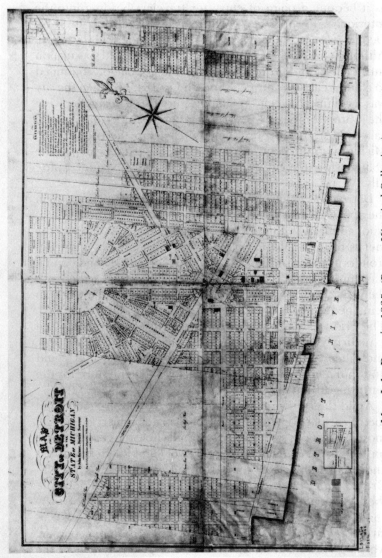

MAP I–1: Detroit, 1835. (*Burton Historical Collection.*)

city, the fashionable elite lived on any number of streets, and the working class resided almost everywhere. Indicative of the city's integrated residential space was Cass Street, Numbers 17–88. Side by side lived three merchants, two architects, a lawyer, a manufacturer, a bookkeeper, three joiners, two turners, two masons, a wagonmaker, a coachmaker, a cabinet-maker, a shipchandler, a blacksmith, two mariners, and two laborers. Embryonic differentiation amid a generally mixed pattern of land use was typical of the American city in the 1760–1840 period.[5]

On the surface, at least, the bustling and changing little city of Detroit appears to have been a disorderly place in the 1830s. Historians can estimate the level of mob violence in modern communities with some precision because serious disturbances generally find their way into the public record. Detroit's newspapers and council journals describe several incidents of mob disorder that took place between 1833 and 1839. Much of this violence was not directly linked to urbanization. Thus, when Detroit blacks twice attacked city authorities in efforts to free runaway slaves who had made their way to the city but were now being returned to their masters in the South, they were acting upon emotions that operated independently of racial tensions in the city itself (though these were great, as a hostile white reaction to the violence suggested). Street disorder between whites and blacks never broke out in Detroit during the 1830s and 1840s. Certainly, white Detroiters did not go "hunting the nigs" as their Philadelphia brethren often did in these years. In 1838, meanwhile, Detroit was also the scene of a number of minor disorders connected entirely with the presence in the city of factions involved in the Canadian civil war, the so-called Patriot's War.[6]

When these disturbances are set aside, however, Detroit emerges as a considerably more orderly city. In July 1835, the xenophobic *Detroit Journal and Advertiser* reported what it described as a "foul disgrace," a disturbance in which twenty or more Irish laborers, who were employed in grading streets near the west end of Jefferson Avenue, assaulted unoffending passers-by, and then routed an informal posse of "worthy citizens" sent to disperse them. The *Journal and Advertiser*, with the election riot in New York City the year before very much on its mind, bemoaned "the gathering of the same materials here that have of late originated the shameless riots in other places." Within a year, Detroit's fashionable young men responded by forming a militia company to protect the city "in times of danger from an outward foe, or internal excitement and turmoils." Nonetheless, the riot had been a relatively tame affair. Nativists, according to the Democrats, had blown it out of proportion, finding a "Riot's Nest" with "nothing in it."[7] If the *Journal and Advertiser* expected to find in the disturbance of 1835 a prelude to regular and more serious group violence in Detroit, it was to be greatly disappointed. There was a minor affray of unclear origin between some Irish and Germans in 1838, while the injection of nativism into political campaign rhetoric in the city during the 1830s and 1840s produced enough scuffles for officials regularly to appoint a few extra constables to keep order at the polls. This was hardly a culture of violence worthy of comparison with New York's, however.[8]

The *Journal and Advertiser* had claimed to be shocked by the "Irish Riot" because in numbers the Irish "were as yet, not sufficiently strong, to break forth in any violent or tumultuous outrage upon the peace and safety of the community." The fact was, Detroit had a growing and visible Irish population. The *Journal and Advertiser* had missed the point. The number of Irish in the city was not as important in affecting the outbreak of violence as their character and residential patterns. Detroit's ethnic and religious groups were not distributed about the city in combustible neighborhood enclaves, which were common in the big eastern cities by the 1830s and 1840s. There were no ethnic clusters of any size, only a few tiny clusters of French and Irish, such as on Wapping Alley, where six of the seven residents were Irish. Generally, the French and the Irish (Germans were few) were spread thin, mixing peacefully with the native-born in almost every quarter of the city. Critical in the residential dispersion of the Irish, the largest ethnic group by the 1840s, were two factors. First, they were settling in a community with an old Catholic tradition and thus met less hostility from the native Protestant population than might otherwise have been the case. Second, many of these

Irish immigrants were of the better sort, "fairly well to do generally," as a prominent Irish resident described them, men of the pre-famine migration, with skills, perhaps a little capital, and enough wherewithal to have made their way to the urban frontier. Consequently, their residential choices as a group were not limited by financial or occupational considerations.[9]

The peaceful tradition of Detroit's early volunteer fire companies illustrates the absence in Detroit during the 1830s and 1840s of group conflict based on the development of contiguous neighborhoods of an ethnic or occupational character. Not a single riot, not even a minor disturbance, marred the record of the volunteers into the 1850s. They were often honored by Detroit's prominent citizens as conscientious men, who displayed "laudable spirit" and acted from "motives of the purest philanthropy." Detroit's firemen contrasted with those of Boston and Philadelphia in the 1830s and 1840s, where the once respectable volunteer companies had degenerated to little more than street gangs, fighting and brawling at every turn. Detroiters often made note of this as they praised their own fire laddies. The bellicosity of these eastern big-city volunteer companies was usually fueled by strong ethnic or occupational identities, in turn promoted by the character of the neighborhoods around which the companies tended to organize. In Detroit, a relatively small and undifferentiated city, the fire companies had not yet become defenders of urban turf. Neighborhood street gangs, who might have used the fire companies for their own purposes, seemed to be all but nonexistent. Detroit's newspapers reveal none of the warfare between gangs with their colorful names that David R. Johnson finds in the *Philadelphia Public Ledger* of the 1840s.[10]

Indeed, the firemen of Detroit were hardly the stuff of which street gangs were made. Charles Hathaway, one of their nineteenth-century chroniclers, says that with "very rare exceptions, the 'best men of the town' belonged to some one of the several fire companies. . . ." The fire stations, he adds, were "the club houses of the day . . . and in the evenings filled with the 'bloods' of the town enjoying social intercourse. . . ." Hathaway's list of the city's firemen in 1844, and an earlier list in the *Detroit Advertiser* in 1839, support his contention, for both

contain the names of some of the most promising and fashionable young men in Detroit. Four future mayors of the city turn
up on the 1844 list alone, an indication not of the role of the
fire companies in an emerging political machine, but of their
role as a requisite social institution for ambitious young men.
Sixty percent of all the names on the 1844 list appear in the
1845 city directory. Two-thirds of these men were shopkeepers and skilled workers, and a healthy sprinkling were
merchants and professionals. Furthermore, there seemed to be
no striking contrasts among the individual companies in their
occupational character, nor their ethnic makeup. A plotting of
the residences of the volunteers shows a few clusters within
companies, but on the whole each company drew members
from throughout the city.[11] It was socializing and service to the
community rather than neighborhood or ethnic interests that
made the fire companies appealing to the volunteers. Detroit's
firemen, contrasting as they did with the gang-oriented and
violent firemen of Philadelphia and other big cities, typified
the still immature and uncomplicated nature of the community—a community whose experience with law and order
inspired such confidence in informal means of control that
people expected the ringing of the bells atop the First Presbyterian Church at nine o'clock every evening to chase all
disorderly persons from the streets.

A CHANGING CITY AND THE PROBLEM OF VICE

Detroit's generally peaceful tradition was shattered in the
1850s, as the benign spatial arrangements of the 1830s and
1840s gave way to more disruptive patterns. The violence of
the 1850s stemmed from the kind of neighborhood concerns
that drove the antirailroad rioters onto Gratiot Street in
1849–50. The neighborhoods involved were a product of
Detroit's booming growth in the decade and a half after 1845,
when the population soared from thirteen to forty-five thousand and the city became a major commercial center.

"The business and prospects of this city were never so flour-
ishing and promising as now," the *Detroit Free Press* claimed in

1851. "There is no department of industry that does not wear an air of enterprize *[sic]*." Already a bustling port, Detroit was linked by rail to Chicago in 1850 and to the east coast by way of Canada in 1853. Many Detroit merchants now concentrated entirely on wholesaling and forwarding, and plank roads stretched fifty miles and more out from the city, drawing the hinterland to the urban marketplace. Although as late as 1860 it still ranked only forty-sixth in manufacturing (even boosters admitted that manufacturing was carried on "in a quiet way"), Detroit was processing enormous quantities of grain, lumber, copper, and iron ore from a Michigan hinterland that now stretched to Lake Superior. In 1851, for example, the city shipped almost nine million feet of sawed pine to Buffalo. More advanced industry was also present. Detroit factories turned out steam engines, even a few railroad locomotives.[12]

In 1853, a Detroit gazetteer boasted that "true fraternization" existed in the city, that it was "an altar at which all the seemingly discordant tongues of religious society may converge."[13] Like many American cities in the late 1840s and early 1850s, Detroit was nearly swamped with foreign immigrants, Germans now as well as Irish. Much of the city's growth in these years was in fact attributable to the arrival of the foreign-born, who made up almost half the total population in Detroit by 1850. A good proportion of the city's new residents, especially the Irish and Germans, and the working class generally, settled in what had been largely unpopulated tracts on the perimeter of the city, beyond Hastings Street on the east side and Third Street on the west. These new areas of single-family dwellings and a few small "tenements" were different from any that Detroit had known previously. More removed and detached from the heart of the city (though still within walking distance), more thoroughly residential in function, and more likely to be identified with an ethnic group, they were really subcommunities, or more precisely neighborhoods, in the classic sense of that term.

The Irish immigrants who began to arrive in Detroit around 1846, just after the potato rot made its first appearance in Ireland, were of a different character from those the city had welcomed before. They were, as JoEllen Vinyard reports in

TABLE I–1: POPULATION BY WARD AND NATIONAL ORIGIN,

	West Side Wards			Central Ward
	1	5	8	2
United States				
White	1,632	1,658	1,056	751
Black	6	4	20	0
Germany	107	99	359	110
Ireland	967	760	1,984	268
England	278	508	565	103
France	63	76	51	34
Scotland	210	111	251	12
Other	40	0	2	14
TOTAL	3,303	3,216	4,288	1,292

Source: *Johnston's Detroit Directory and Business Advertiser* (Detroit: George

her study of the Detroit Irish, less well educated, less skilled, and certainly less well off. The occupational status of these newer immigrants demonstrates this. In 1850, Irish heads of household in Detroit who had left the old country with the great famine were twice as likely to be common laborers as those who had emigrated before 1846.[14] The generally dispersed pattern of Irish residence now began to give way to greater concentration, as the newcomers poured into the city and sought out cheap living space, preferably amid their countrymen. Table I–1, based on a private census taken in 1853 by the compiler of the city directory, shows the heavy concentration of Irish on Detroit's west side. The area around Michigan Avenue in the Eighth Ward acquired the popular name "Corktown" about this time and was emerging as the focal point of the Irish community. An old Irish Catholic church in the central part of the city was even lifted off its foundations and moved a full fifteen blocks to Corktown in 1849.[15]

The Irish were Detroit's largest foreign-born group as late as 1850, but this was soon to change. Germans were arriving in the city at a rapid rate, and it was not long before they had

1853

	East Side Wards			Total
3	4	6	7	
1,337	776	1,574	955	9,759
103	272	86	42	533
605	2,062	1,465	2,557	7,364
658	548	351	326	5,862
325	238	532	213	2,762
335	550	461	655	2,225
79	45	238	49	995
55	38	17	118	284
3,517	4,529	4,724	4,915	29,784

E. Pomeroy, 1853), p. xiv.

surpassed the Irish in numbers and were close to overtaking the native-born. Unlike the Irish, and perhaps mostly because of the insecurity they felt as a non-English-speaking group, nearly all Detroit's Germans settled near one another. In the 1850s, over 90 percent of them lived on the east side, particularly in the area between Jefferson and Gratiot in the Fourth and Seventh wards (Table I–1). The *Detroit Advertiser* painted a romantic picture of the east-side German neighborhoods in 1859:

Almost every German who lives in that part of the city can and does sit under his own vine, if not under his own fig tree; and it is a pleasing sight on a pleasant summer's evening, to see so many who have left the Faderland for this, the land of their choice, gathered together under the vine planted by their own hands—the male adults of the families puffing away at their meerschaums, drinking their lager, or sipping their Rhine-wein, while the mothers keep an eye to their little ones who are tumbling about in the grass at their feet.[16]

If this description was an idealized one, it was nonetheless indicative of how much Detroit's German neighborhoods stood out in the city's changing spatial mosaic.

TABLE I-2: DISTRIBUTION BY WARD OF SMALL WORKSHOPS

| | West Side Wards | | | |
	1	5	8	9ª
"Mechanic shops"	43	46	10	13
Bars for the retail of spirituous liquors, wine, and beer	89	33	38	20

ªCreated in 1857. Other ward boundaries remained the same.
SOURCE: *Rept. Water Comm.* (1857), pp. 53-54.

Our understanding of the German subcommunity in the nineteenth-century American city has been enhanced recently by Kathleen Conzen's superb study of Milwaukee. She demonstrates convincingly that Milwaukee's Germans, much more so than its Irish, experienced nothing like the classic model of immigrant disorientation and disorganization portrayed in such studies as Oscar Handlin's *The Uprooted*. Instead, the Germans created "a miniature society independent of the host community"—a self-contained, complex, largely self-supporting, self-servicing, and culturally secure subcommunity that made for a relatively easy adjustment to the new environment, and a quite satisfying and happy existence. Milwaukee, of course, was exceptional in its sheer numbers of Germans. The heavily German neighborhoods were so extensive there that they had their own "downtown." Nonetheless, there were a number of cities in the Ohio Valley and Great Lakes region, including Detroit, that shared the general urban experience and heavy German immigration of Milwaukee and whose German neighborhoods were undoubtedly similar.[17]

There was certainly much about Detroit's German neighborhoods that set them apart from other immigrant neighborhoods in the city. For example, data collected by JoEllen Vinyard from the 1850 census reveals that Detroit's Germans were more occupationally diverse than the Irish. One of three German male heads of household was a skilled craftsman, compared with only one of six among the Irish. At the same time, as

AND RETAIL LIQUOR ESTABLISHMENTS, 1857

Central Ward			East Side Wards			Total
2	3	4	6	7	10ᵃ	
114	61	44	32	53	5	421
74	83	74	27	65	21	524

Table I–2 shows, most of the city's small workshops outside the central ward were on the east side. So while the many Irish laborers (half of all male household heads in 1850) left Corktown to work on the docks or in the factories and mills that dotted the riverfront from one end of the city to the other, the typical German artisan was likely to pursue his craft in or at least near his own neighborhood, perhaps even in a shop adjacent to his home. Also, while the native-born in Detroit owned the most and best real estate, in the city, property ownership was actually most evenly distributed among the Germans, according to Vinyard's data, and this would enhance their attachment to the neighborhood. Finally, there were many saloons and beer halls on the German east side (Table I–2). The neighborhood pub among working-class groups has traditionally been a vital and indispensable institution, serving as a focal point, a place for neighborhood residents to meet and socialize or to discuss matters of local import. The German beer hall, in particular, reinforced ethnic identity.[18]

The German sections on Detroit's east side in the 1850s resemble in many ways the classic working-class city neighborhoods described by modern sociologists. It would appear especially appropriate to compare them to the still vital inner-city ethnic neighborhoods Andrew Greeley has studied. Greeley points to the intricate relationship between social turf and the meaning of ethnicity. In this respect he shares the belief of Gerald Suttles that urbanites are ever cognizant of the physical city around them, which they delineate, perhaps with some exaggeration, into segments good and evil, friendly and hos-

tile, safe and unsafe. In defending their neighborhoods from
outside interference, ethnic groups defend the spatial identity
that gives meaning to the ethnic one. "A threat to the home and
the neighborhood," writes Greeley of the ethnic, "is a threat to
the very core of his personality."[19] The German neighborhoods
of Detroit in the 1850s faced just such a threat, though it was
one they imposed on themselves through their own rapid
expansion. The problem was that parts of the city's east side
were filled with bawdy houses of prostitution. As a matter of
neighborhood concern, brothels were far more serious than
railroad tracks. Consequently, they provoked neighborhood
disorder to which the Gratiot Street incidents of 1849–50 paled
in comparison.

During the 1830s and 1840s, brothels had only once been
the source of any public controversy in Detroit. This was in
1841. A black man named James Slaughter and his white
mistress, Peg Welch, operated a brothel on the street directly
behind City Hall in the center of the city. It was certainly not
the only house of prostitution in Detroit, nor the most disorderly, but its conspicuous location had brought it to the
attention of the Common Council, particularly the obstrep-
erous chairman of its Committee on Health, Joseph H. Bagg.
Bagg denounced the brothel as the most notorious in the city
and the breeding ground of crime. Three years earlier, the city
had let Slaughter off the hook after he lost a suit filed by a
group of citizens. This time, officials were determined to see
the matter through. They ordered the city marshal to tear the
brothel down, an order he promptly obeyed. Both Slaughter
and Welch then filed their own suits against the city, and both
had the satisfaction of seeing the State Supreme Court rule in
their favor. "It must, indeed, be an extreme case," the judges
observed, "that will authorize the municipal authorities of the
city to doom a house to destruction by a simple resolution
declaring it a house of ill fame."[20] The action of the city may
have been hasty and improper, but it had certainly solved the
problem for those concerned about it. Slaughter and Welch
did not return to their old roost. In the meantime, the city's
houses of prostitution kept a low profile during the 1840s,

perhaps to escape the wrath of municipal authority as it had been exhibited in 1841.

By the 1850s, however, the city's rapid growth and changing spatial patterns had created an entirely new environment. No longer were brothels and those offended by them able to keep out of each other's way. Detroit's brothels were not as multifarious as those described in Sanger's famous New York survey of 1858.[21] There were high-class and low-class places. The city's fashionable bordellos were discreetly operated in and around the central part of the city, particularly on the west side near the river. The less pretentious places, and of those there were far more, tended to locate throughout Detroit's east side. There were a few on the riverfront, but most were situated between Congress and Gratiot streets. The largest concentration of brothels straddled the tracks of the Detroit & Milwaukee Railroad (the old Detroit & Pontiac) on Dequindre Street, which was the city's eastern boundary until the Tenth Ward was added in 1857. These brothels had no doubt located there originally to avoid municipal authority, but they also had the advantage of being visible to railroad workers and travelers as the trains slowed to a crawl to negotiate a curve near the river.[22]

Many of the areas in which vice established a foothold had been relatively unsettled until the early 1850s. Now they were precisely those areas coveted for residential space by the working class, particularly the Germans. As the brothels became less isolated they became more controversial. The competition for space produced considerable tension. To be sure, not all Germans were repelled by prostitution. German males surely frequented brothels, just as surely as German females were counted among the prostitutes. German musicians often performed in the dance houses that doubled as brothels. Nevertheless, brothels could pose a threat to what the Germans above all others on the east side were trying to create in the way of neighborhood life. Prostitutes and their customers were bad examples for children. Bordellos offered temptations that could destroy families. They undermined property values. Most of all, brothels affronted their neighbors because many of them catered to an interracial clientele.

Houses of prostitution in other parts of the city often refused to admit blacks. For example, black sailors and dockworkers were turned away from houses along the riverfront and forced "uptown" to the brothels on the outer east side. Moreover, Detroit's black population, small though it was, concentrated on the city's east side, as Table I–1 indicates, so German settlement coincided with black settlement. As German neighborhoods spread to the outer east side during the mid-1850s, they also moved away from the principal areas of black residence. That many of the brothels, particularly those on the edge of the city near the tracks, catered to blacks not only offended the sensibility of Germans to "amalgamated" sexual relations, but also may have aroused fears of a possible extension of black settlement into their most homogeneous and self-conscious neighborhoods.

How the immigrant working class, and the Germans in particular, were to respond to the problem of vice on the east side had a lot to do with problems they faced from other quarters. The hostility native-born Americans in many parts of the country showed toward the European immigrants who poured into the cities at mid-century was evident in Detroit as well. It emerged in a bitter controversy over public schools that tore the city apart at its political seams in 1853. Catholics wanted tax money to support their own schools, or else special consideration given to Catholic children in the public schools. The city's Protestant leaders, the native-born especially, would have nothing of the sort and vigorously opposed the idea. Although the Irish were the most directly involved in the issue, Germans could not help but see in the episode a larger nativist feeling rising to the surface in Detroit.[23]

They did not have to wait long to see further evidence of native hostility. In 1853, the Michigan legislature passed a tough liquor measure modeled after the infamous "Maine Law." Thanks to the strength of the Democratic party in the city, the new law went largely unenforced in Detroit. Temperance advocates were furious, and they generated enough political strength in 1856 to help elect a sympathetic Republican mayor. The agitation of liquor reformers prompted the periodic harassment of saloonkeepers by the sheriff's deputies, who willing as they were to let the state law remain a dead letter, tried to draw the line at Sunday drinking. Even the Democratic, antitemperance police justice was a sabbatarian.[24] For many immigrants, particularly Germans, the "Continental Sunday" was an indispensable tradition. Detroit's beer gardens were filled to capacity on Sunday afternoons with crowds of Germans enjoying their lager, singing and dancing to the music of the old country. Germans reacted sharply to the temperance movement, which was dominated by native-born Protestants, as an attack on legitimate immigrant customs. They were in the forefront of the protests against the state's liquor law, and they offered impassioned opposition to sabbatarianism. In 1856, a crowd of two hundred people, mostly Germans, gathered angrily outside the courthouse during the trial of one of their countrymen who had been arrested for keeping his saloon open on Sunday. The new protemperance mayor added insult to injury by calling out a recently organized nativist militia company to watch the crowd. Detroit came very close to having the kind of serious clash between Germans and the authorities over liquor policy that Chicago had the year before and New York had the next.[25]

As if all this were not enough, Detroit's economy became sluggish in the mid–1850s, when the city grew at a much slower rate than it had in the 1847–53 boom period, and then when it felt the economic shock waves from the national depression of 1857. Detroit's unemployment rose, and immigrant workers fared badly, not only Irish and German casual laborers, but also craftsmen. German carpenters, for example, suffered from the severe drop-off in construction throughout the city. In the spring of 1858, crowds of unemployed workingmen— some Irish but mostly Germans—twice marched on City Hall demanding public works projects that would provide them with jobs. City officials were not receptive to the idea. The press told the men to leave the city and look for work in the countryside.[26] These setbacks were compounded by the economic threat the temperance movement posed to the German community. Not only did the many tavernkeepers stand to lose from rigid liquor controls, so did brewery owners and their workers. Fifteen of the twenty-three breweries in Detroit in

1857 were located in the German wards. Most of these were operated by Germans who no doubt employed German labor. Of the twenty-eight breweries listed in the 1862 city directory, sixteen had German proprietors.[27]

So as the city's German neighborhoods faced the problem of vice, they were reeling from cultural and economic blows. If houses of prostitution were undesirable features of an area in which people hoped to establish stable, family oriented neighborhoods, they could also become targets for people seeking to release the tensions built up by threats to their customs and their livelihood.

In June 1853, a petition came to the Common Council from the "residents of Macomb Street" on the city's east side, calling for the suppression of houses of ill fame on that street. Similar petitions from residents in other parts of the Seventh and Tenth wards followed over the next few years. The names of only two petitioners were recorded in the journals of the Common Council: Charles Perry (misspelled Perez), a physician from the Fourth Ward, and John Roberts, a laborer who resided in the Tenth Ward. Otherwise, all that is certain is that the petitioners were residents of the outer east side, and that their principal concerns were the "negro houses of ill fame" on Lafayette and adjacent streets in the vicinity of the Detroit & Milwaukee tracks. Yet the petitions came from the area of the city most heavily settled by Germans. That the first names to appear on two of the petitions were not German does not make it improbable that many of the rest of the names were.[28]

City officials responded civilly and promptly to the petitions, if not exactly enthusiastically. A special Common Council committee agreed that brothels lowered surrounding property values and otherwise harmed neighborhood life. Officials talked of toughening the ordinances against disorderly houses already on the books and enforcing them more rigorously. On the whole, the city side-stepped the issue, paying lip service to the interests of neighborhood residents, while in the end recommending nothing more in the way of a final solution to the problem than that residents file complaints and let the courts handle the matter.[29] It would only be after mobs took the matter into their own hands, in fact, that the city attorney ordered (and led) the first full-scale "descent" on outer east-side brothels.[30]

Clearly the city was not about to condemn the brothels as public nuisances and tear them down, which the petitioners no doubt would have liked. Officials appeared sensitive to the legal implications and were probably conversant with the details of the 1841 affair and its embarrassing denouement. Then too, Oliver M. Hyde, a Whig-Republican with pro-temperance and nativist support, was the mayor of Detroit in 1854–55 and again during what would prove to be the crucial year of the brothel crisis, 1856–57. It was Hyde who called out the militia, perhaps unnecessarily and provocatively, in the midst of the controversial trial involving the German tavern-keeper in 1856. "A German" writing to the *Free Press* on that occasion claimed that Hyde and his supporters habitually referred to Germans as "Teutonic Bullies." This may have been more rumor than fact. Nevertheless, Hyde was likely not to be particularly receptive to complaints about brothels from mostly German neighborhoods.[31] Indeed, the German voice in city government was weak, although the Democrats, whom the German wards consistently supported, were generally success-ful at the aldermanic level. Only three of forty-nine men serving on the Common Council from 1853 to 1860 had German names.[32] Finally, and perhaps most importantly, the concern about the brothels was confined to the outer parts of the city. Unlike the bawdy house of Slaughter and Welch in 1841, these brothels were not located near valuable property and the residences of prominent citizens, but instead afflicted peripheral working-class neighborhoods. It was not a matter that would likely produce another fashionable crusader like Alderman Bagg and a tenacious Common Council.

That the municipality did not respond to their complaints was more than a little irritating to the residents on Detroit's east side as they discussed the matter around tables in their taverns and beer halls, or across the benches at their workshops. Here was a city government, so it would seem to them, no more willing to deal forcefully with a serious threat to the vitality and morality of their neighborhoods than it was to deal sympa-thetically with their legitimate social customs. Apparently brothels could stay, beer halls and pubs could not. The best solution seemed obvious. Neighborhood residents would tear the brothels down themselves and chase away the prostitutes, their madams, and their black customers.

VIOLENCE AND SPATIAL HEGEMONY

The "whorehouse riot," common enough in eighteenth-century American communities, was an especially frequent occurrence in the middle years of the nineteenth century. Boston, St. Louis, Louisville, Washington, Minneapolis, Kansas City, and New York were only some of the cities where antiprostitution violence took place between 1820 and 1870.[33] The use of violence to control vice was not a new tactic in Detroit by the late 1850s. The Common Council had employed it in 1841 under the guise of legal authority, and ordinary citizens occasionally and for a variety of reasons assaulted houses of ill fame in the city. In 1834, one of James Slaughter's places, in fact, was visited by a stone-throwing mob of local residents. In 1847, small crowds attacked another brothel twice in one week, though the location of the house was not reported and the purpose of the attacks is unclear. Equally uncertain is what provoked a gang of white men to ransack a bordello located in the heart of the city in 1852, but the fact that its "abandoned white women" catered to blacks was no doubt critical. Integrated brothels were expected to stay out of the downtown.[34] It seems likely that all these incidents had something to do with the concerns of the people living or doing business in the vicinity of the brothels about the character of these places and the elements to whom they appealed. They were isolated incidents, however, usually resulting in only minor damage to the brothels in question. The problem of vice in the residential neighborhoods on the outer east side, on the other hand, was of unprecedented proportions and emotional content. It would be productive of considerably more concerted and destructive violence.

Beginning in the summer of 1855 and continuing every summer through 1859, one bordello after another felt the fury of an angry mob. There were twelve major incidents in all, and at least seventeen brothels were either seriously damaged or completely destroyed. The violence took place entirely on the city's east side more specifically, in the upper part of the Fourth Ward near Gratiot Street, along Hastings Street in the Sixth Ward, and all along the Detroit & Milwaukee tracks in the Seventh and Tenth wards. The brothels attacked were invariably of the lowest class, often places catering to blacks and employing white prostitutes. The number of rioters in most incidents was about fifty to one hundred, though occasionally it may have reached as high as two or three hundred. The mobs almost always acted under cover of darkness, meeting at a rendezvous first, and then moving swiftly to prearranged targets. The prostitutes and other "inmates" were usually warned to vacate the building. The furniture was then ripped up or dragged out into the street and the windows broken. If the rioters were determined to destroy the place, they would apply the torch to the battered building. The mobs were disciplined and discriminating. According to one report, they showed a "regular organization." One is reminded of the careful and systematic anti-abolition mobs Leonard Richards finds at work in a number of towns and cities in the 1830s.[35]

The most tumultuous summer was in 1857. Involved were the houses of prostitution along the railroad tracks in the Tenth Ward on the outer east side, the area of vice that provoked more violence than anywhere else. In late June, a mob burned or ransacked six brothels on Lafayette Street in that ward. It was easily the most daring and concerted effort against vice by neighborhood residents that Detroit had yet witnessed. "These citizens," wrote the *Detroit Tribune*, "having appealed to the Council for protection in vain, and having been refused, took the law into their own hands." The violence prompted the Common Council to form a special committee (no aldermen from the Tenth Ward, or even the Seventh Ward, were on the committee, however) to look into the matter of the brothels along the tracks and to hear complaints from local residents. It was this committee that agreed with the complainants about the harmful effects of vice on surrounding neighborhoods but could recommend nothing more than an effort by local residents to get the keepers of the houses arrested under the laws against disorderly places.[36] So, within a week a handbill appeared on fences and walls throughout the Tenth Ward giving notice "that all the houses of ill fame must be removed from the 7th and 10th Wards within thirty days, or they will have a visit from a Vigilance Committee of twelve hundred men who are organized for the purpose, and are determined to remove the nuisance by force unless the same is done peaceably before that time expires."[37] The residents of the ward were indeed determined. Even the city attorney's raid on some of the brothels a week and a half later did not mollify them. On July 17, the *Advertiser* reported that the Vigilance Committee had met and was still prepared to act with force. Exactly two weeks later, its relationship to the Vigilance Committee unclear, a mob formed in the lower part of the Tenth Ward, apparently intent on starting there and working its way up the railroad tracks. The rioters attacked two houses before a school inspector and a Seventh Ward alderman intervened. The arrival on the scene of the fire companies scattered the crowd. There were rumors of imminent vigilante activity a month or so later, but the summer's violence had finally ended.

Who was responsible for the disorders of 1855–59? This is difficult to establish, since there were seldom any arrests, for reasons to be examined shortly. In one case, in 1855, officers arrested not rioters but the blacks whose dance hall had been attacked. In 1856, four men with what appear to be Irish names were arrested for throwing stones at a brothel in an unreported location, though the only arrestee who could be identified, a sailor named James Gregory, lived in Corktown, so perhaps the incident involved one of the few brothels on the west side. Eight more men, again with Irish names, were arrested in connection with the violence just described in the lower Tenth Ward in early August 1857. Only three could be positively identified, and two, a boilermaker and a laborer, lived in the immediate vicinity of the brothel attacked. The other, an architect, boarded downtown. A fourth was either a printer from Corktown or a moulder who lived about ten blocks from the scene of the riot, probably the latter.[38] That the rioters tended to live near the brothels they were attacking is substantiated by newspaper reports, which consistently stated or implied as much. It seems unlikely, however, that most rioters were Irish. On a number of occasions the two major dailies described the mobs in no uncertain terms as German. A black arrested after one of the riots for sporting a pistol said he needed it to protect himself from "the Dutch."[39] Most of the violence took place in and around the most heavily populated German areas in the city, and it is likely that Germans were prominent in the mobs. The eight Irishmen arrested in 1857, furthermore, were connected with the only serious incident that occurred near the river and on the periphery of the principal German neighborhoods.

Whatever the case, the rioting was a splendid success from the standpoint of the offended neighborhood residents. The first wave of mobbism in 1856 and 1857 drove many of the prostitutes from the outer east side. Some of them returned during 1858, but the final display of violence in the summer of 1859 sent them scampering for good. By 1860, the vice quarters along the tracks had been broken up completely and the areas absorbed into the residential neighborhoods that surrounded them. When the rubble of what were once some of the most bawdy houses in the city had been cleared away, several of the blocks were built over with "tenements"—probably small two- and three-family dwellings—housing workers employed in the factories and workshops along the riverfront.[40] At the same time, the other vice districts in the Fourth, Sixth, and Seventh wards were thinned out considerably. The most objectionable of the houses were certainly gone or forced to operate more discreetly. Only a few scattered incidents of violence against brothels lingered into the 1860s.[41]

If the disorders of 1855–59 eliminated vice in many parts of the east side, they also exposed the inadequacy of Detroit's police arrangements. The job of preserving order in the city rested principally upon the shoulders of the county sheriff and the ten or so deputies he appointed to handle criminal business in Detroit. There was no regular night watch, only a fire watch in the steeple of one of the city's churches. In addition, ten constables, one elected by each ward, were empowered to make criminal arrests. Neither the deputies nor the constables, however, patrolled the city on a routine basis, and only with great difficulty could they be assembled in a body. The deputies, especially veteran reappointees, were quite good at tracking down criminals and returning stolen goods, but they had little experience, or even interest in, handling street crowds. In general, the city's police officers seemed to be reacting, always a step behind, during the brothel disorders. The riots almost invariably managed to catch them off guard, even though in some instances the violence was publicly anticipated. The show of police force was most impressive only in the wake of disorder. The deputies seemed best able to prevent follow-up violence, not the initial outburst. Thus, as noted already, a school inspector and an alderman were in one incident the only officials on hand to deal with the mobs. Not a single rioter was arrested at the scene of any of the major riots. Admittedly, much of the disorder was the work of highly organized, clandestine crowds in peripheral sections of the city. Officers had a tough chore. Nevertheless, Detroit's police performed spottily throughout the crisis.

On the other hand, how committed *were* officials to keeping order in the neighborhoods? The evidence would suggest not very committed at all. The mayor and Common Council had not been disposed to intervene on behalf of neighborhood petitioners, and they seemed equally indisposed to intervene to prevent the neighborhoods from taking matters into their own hands. Mayor Hyde at one point visited several of the brothels along the tracks, taking with him one of the Vigilance Committee's handbills to advise the prostitutes of what would happen to them if they did not leave the area. The *Free Press,* always looking for the opportunity to jump on the Republican mayor, was aghast at what it felt was Hyde's pandering to mob rule. "The keepers of disorderly houses," it exclaimed, "are not wild beasts, to be hunted down and exterminated with fire and sword."[42] The mayor apparently felt that he would rather help scare the prostitutes away than find himself in the difficult position of having to send a municipal force into such a highly charged situation. His controversial decision the year before to call out the militia to intimidate the German antisabbatarians may have been on his mind. In the meantime, some of the city government's own were occasionally joining the mobs. Unnamed "city officers" were reportedly involved in one riot in the Fourth Ward, while a Tenth Ward constable appears to have encouraged some of the disorder in that ward.[43] The deputies seemed uninterested in pursuing any leads in the arrest of rioters. The eight men apprehended in connection with the violence in August 1857 were arrested primarily because of the determined prodding of one of the alleged brothelkeepers whose place had been attacked. Then, they were acquitted when the city's prosecuting attorney presented a lackadaisical argument in the courtroom.[44]

Thus the violence of 1855–59 may have been a crisis in group relations and spatial development, but it was not a crisis in law and order. There were the obligatory expressions of concern in the press about mobbism in the city's streets, spliced with the inevitable partisan political rhetoric. The rioting prompted little debate, however, over the matter of the city's policing and the dilemma of order-keeping in a growing and changing community. Such a debate was in fact already underway and moving toward a climax. Its focus, however, was not on the residential outskirts but on the heart of the city, where a spatial transformation of profound consequences was taking place.

TWO

The New Downtown

The growing neighborhoods of working-class immigrants on Detroit's east and west sides were but one feature of the city's new spatial differentiation in the 1850s and 1860s, a differentiation that replaced the generally mixed and undefined pattern of land use that had characterized the city before. In addition to the mostly residential periphery, a substantial and, to many in the city, an impressive central business district formed, symbolic of Detroit's growth and progress. The men whose capital built the new business district or on whose real estate it rested joined with fashionable lawyers and other prominent citizens to develop prestigious residential neighborhoods immediately adjacent to the business district on the near west side. Where these fashionable areas met the business district near the river, but especially on the other side of the business district to the east, a wholly different environment emerged. Here a highly transient, mostly unattached population of young, working-class males crowded into boarding houses and cheap hotels. Around them grew up the many places of amusement they found necessary and appealing, particularly brothels and saloons. It was, in all, a spatial mosaic of striking contrasts, a setting that dramatized the social and economic diversity of the city.

THE CENTRAL BUSINESS DISTRICT

"There has been, unquestionably, no period in the history of Detroit," the compiler of the city directory boasted in 1852, "so

32

strongly marked with unmistakable signs of rapid growth and permanent prosperity as have the past three or four years." As it was for the emergence of Detroit's outer residential neighborhoods, the boom period of the late 1840s and early 1850s was critical in redesigning the city's central and riverfront areas. The old hodgepodge of stores, shops, homes, and vacant lots that had met the eye even along parts of such principal business streets as Jefferson and Woodward in the years before 1845 now gave way to a solid central business district encompassing forty blocks by the 1860s. The transformation was most visible in the switch from frame to brick construction. As of the late 1840s, there was not "an unbroken front of substantial brick stores on a single square in the city," according to the 1852 directory. This soon changed, as new brick "business blocks" began to rise all over the heart of the city. By 1861, 80 percent of the buildings in the Second Ward were of brick or stone. The newspapers followed the progress of this construction in enthusiastic, magniloquent, block-by-block descriptions, noting how the new brick buildings would be "a great addition" or a "substantial improvement" to this or that street. At first the buildings were architecturally disappointing. "The extraordinary demand for these buildings, and the haste with which they have been erected," the *Free Press* explained in May 1851, "will probably account for the great similarity and plainness of fronts." The utilitarian designs became less and less satisfactory to a business community that was committed to the growth and progress of Detroit. People wanted a truly impressive commercial center. Over the next few years business architecture came of age in Detroit and matched the city's expectations. Buildings were now constructed in the "most approved" and "modern" styles, as the once drab quarters of business sported Italianate cornices and cast-iron pilasters.[1]

The shift to brick construction in the heart of the city was not just for show. There were practical considerations. In 1848, flames swept through several blocks not far from the commercial center of the city at the convergence of Jefferson and Woodward avenues. The fire was another lesson in the hazards of frame construction, and the area was rebuilt almost entirely in brick, setting the pace for the rest of the business district. In the meantime, the growing numbers of merchants who were

engaged exclusively in wholesaling needed larger and sturdier
quarters for their operations than even the most successful retail-wholesale merchant had required in the 1830s and 1840s,
and this made practical the use of brick. Zachariah Chandler,
later to be an important national figure in the Republican
party, ran Detroit's largest jobbing house in the early 1850s.
His business was housed in a four-story brick edifice with ten
rooms of twenty-five hundred square feet apiece.[2]

The latest urban amenities enhanced the progressive and
more substantial air of the heart of the city. "If ever a poor unfortunate city was turned up with drains & sewers & laying of
water and gass [sic] pipes," wrote one Detroiter in 1851, "ours
would seem to be the city. . . . But won't we have a fine city
when all these things are finished." The new gas lamps graced
the principal commercial streets downtown. During the 1850s
many of the same streets received a cobblestone covering that
improved considerably upon the muddy, rutted surfaces Detroiters had to negotiate before. By the early 1860s, flagstone
sidewalks were also common.[3]

The development of the central business district had been
given added impetus in the late 1840s when, after efforts by
Detroit merchants and inducements from the Common Council in the form of property-tax breaks, the Michigan Central
Railroad decided to build its new Detroit terminus in the heart
of the city at the western end of Jefferson Avenue. The massive
complex included a wharf, freight depot, passenger terminal,
engine house, and repair shops. The city was ecstatic with its
new additions. "They are an ornament, and a credit to our city
and State," exulted the *Free Press*. The ensemble, especially its
neoclassical passenger station and distinctive domed engine
house, quickly became one of the city's best-known land-
marks.[4]

The railroad complex drew the business district into the
lower west side. A number of big retail-wholesale stores located
in the area soon after the trains started rolling in and out. Shippers, forwarding merchants, and grain dealers built their
warehouses along the river adjacent to the depot, and Front
Street was planked with wood to carry the weight of loaded
wagons making the constant trips from the freight cars. These

were years when the railroad and the lake steamer comple-
mented each other in the flow of goods and produce. Only in
the 1870s did the major rail lines begin to limit the role of the
steamer. Until then, the warehouses of the shippers dominated the riverfront. The preemption of shoreline space by
warehouses was typical of young western cities at an early stage
of their growth, since the railroad was in a better position to af-
fect land use there than in the older eastern cities where waterfront development was already generations old.[5]

Map II–1 is a remarkably detailed building-by-building view
of Detroit in 1853. In it one can see the central business district
beginning to take shape, anchored by the brick "business
blocks" along Jefferson and Woodward avenues. The ware-

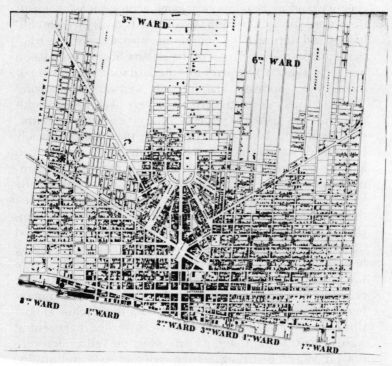

Map II–1: Detroit, 1853. *(Burton Historical Collection.)*

houses lining the riverfront, particularly near the Michigan Central depot, are clearly visible. The entire area was filling in rapidly by this date, and it served as the axis on which other spatial developments in the heart of the city turned.[6]

THE BACHELOR-TRANSIENT SUBCULTURE

The great bulk of Detroit's jobs in the 1850s and 1860s were to be found at the stores, offices, workshops, warehouses, hotels, depots, and landings of the central business district. Many of the men employed downtown were family men who owned or rented single-family dwellings in the working-class neighborhoods beyond the central part of the city. Others, especially single and unattached adult men, were interested in simpler, cheaper, and more temporary living arrangements. Some of these were young men from Detroit who had left their parents' homes and were striking out on their own. Others were transients and in-migrants, part of the massive floating population that gave a special character to American society in this era of immigration, industrialization, and westward expansion.[7] These transient or unattached males were likely to board with other families in the city, especially near the downtown.[8] However, in the very heart of the city, where the number of family households was declining in the mid-nineteenth century, men looking for temporary living space could turn to formal boarding houses and cheap hotels. Most of these were conveniently located in the busiest parts of town, and they often provided their patrons with the right combination of domesticity, companionship, and personal independence. In the boom period of the late 1840s and early 1850s, the number of boarding houses in Detroit grew to well over one hundred. The figure was much lower in the depressed late 1850s. In the next decade boarding houses again proliferated, so that by 1868 they numbered almost two hundred. Throughout these years, at least three of every five boarding houses were situated in the central wards (First, Second, and Third), while the remainder were not far away.[9] Boarding houses varied in style and quality. Some were neat, comfortable places run by motherly widows.

Others were cramped and filthy, especially the tough riverfront saloons that offered cheap, backroom "cribs." In all,
boarding houses were a prominent feature of Detroit's mid-
nineteenth-century scene, just as they were in every city—a
part of urban life that has become almost extinct today.

The hotel and boarding-house population was substantial—
one out of every seven inhabitants of the city according to the
special census taken in 1853 by the compiler of the city directory. This gave the downtown a distinct demographic character. In 1854, there were as many unmarried adults as married
ones living in the three central wards, while in the other wards
the ratio was only one to three.[10] For a closer look at a segment
of the boarding-house population, we can turn to the manuscript census schedules of 1850, 1860, and 1870, and data on
all the persons living in places listed in the schedules as boarding houses or in places where the household head's occupation
was "boarding-house keeper." The data come from the city's
First and Third wards on the near west and east sides,
respectively. These two wards generally contained at least half
of all the boarding houses in Detroit. It should be noted here
that this procedure captures mostly places that were formally
recognized as boarding houses. It is not likely to pick up any of
the numerous saloons that took in boarders, and therefore
perhaps understates the least "respectable" elements in the
total boarding-house population.

As Table II–1 indicates, almost 60 percent of the boarders in
1850 and 1860 were persons living in boarding houses with no
one else of the same surname. By 1870, it was up to 75 percent.
Of these unattached persons, the overwhelming majority were
males, so that by 1870 three out of every five boarders were unattached males (a percentage that was no doubt much higher in
the saloon boarding houses). Table II–2 shows that most of
these unattached male boarders were manual workers, though
an increasing percentage were store or office clerks and other
low-level white-collar employees. Consistently 80 percent or
more were between twenty and forty years of age.

Individual boarding houses tended to take in a variety of
boarders. Samuel Barrett's boarding house on Gratiot and
Brush streets in 1850 was unique. It had twelve boarders, all

TABLE II–1: BOARDING-HOUSE POPULATION, FIRST AND

	First	1850 Third	Total
Boarding houses[a]	15	3	18
Boarders[b]	117	45	162
Boarders per house	7.8	15.0	9.0
Percent unattached[c]	59	60	59
Percent unattached males	44	51	46

[a]All dwellings described by enumerator in margin as boarding houses, or for which the household head was listed as "boarding-house keeper."
[b]All persons living in boarding house except boarding-house keeper and persons with same surname, or if no one listed as boarding-house keeper, then first person listed and all persons with same surname.

TABLE II–2: PERCENTAGE DISTRIBUTION OF UNATTACHED FIRST AND THIRD WARDS, 1850, 1860, 1870

	First	1850 Third	Total
Professional/proprietor	0	13	4
White collar[a]	10	4	8
Skilled	67	78	71
Semiskilled/unskilled	21	0	15
None/other	2	4	3
Under 20 years	8	9	8
20–29	67	43	60
30–39	19	35	24
40 and over	6	13	8

[a]Includes all "clerks."
SOURCE: Manuscript federal census schedules (microfilm), Detroit, 1850, 1860, 1870.

THIRD WARDS, 1850, 1860, 1870

First	1860 Third	Total	First	1870 Third	Total
25	8	33	25	46	71
226	133	359	205	499	704
9.0	16.6	10.6	8.2	10.8	9.9
50	66	56	69	77	75
42	52	45	53	62	59

eAll boarders in boarding house with no other person of same surname.
SOURCE: Manuscript federal census schedules (microfilm), Detroit, 1850, 1860, 1870.

MALES IN BOARDING HOUSES BY OCCUPATION AND AGE,

First	1860 Third	Total	First	1870 Third	Total
12	14	13	11	4	6
16	30	22	28	25	25
36	38	37	32	52	47
31	12	23	25	17	19
5	6	6	4	3	3
9	6	7	3	11	9
56	71	63	63	62	62
20	22	21	21	21	21
15	1	9	13	6	8

brickmakers. Almost as unusual was James McDonald's, which in 1860 included fourteen sailors and three fishermen among its twenty-seven boarders. More typical was Horace Sweet's boarding house on Randolph Street in the Third Ward in 1870. Its ten boarders—eight males and two females, mostly in their twenties—included six manual workers, two store clerks, a bookkeeper, and a servant. Only the occupationally elite boarders tended to cluster. Most of them could be found in just a few boarding houses, such as Daniel Rabineau's in the fashionable First Ward in 1860. When the census-taker passed his way, a grocer, a lawyer, an editor, an architect, and three female teachers were among his twelve boarders.

The transient and unattached males—young lawyers, traveling businessmen, petty clerks, hotel waiters, and manual workers of all kinds—who lived in boarding houses and other places in and around the downtown helped create a "bachelor subculture" of considerable proportions in Detroit, as elsewhere in nineteenth-century urban America.[11] These men formed a subcommunity based on mutual interests and needs. In the process, they helped to shape, spawn, and sustain a number of downtown urban amusements, which became, in addition to the boarding houses themselves, the most visible features of their subculture. To be sure, married men with families who were more or less "permanent" residents of the city could and did patronize these places of amusement, especially if they worked downtown, but it was primarily to the unattached "men in motion" living in the heart of the city that the amusements owed their growing popularity. These were institutions that had to accommodate themselves to the confined space of the inner city, to the constant turnover among their enthusiasts, and to the regulated daily time of an urban work force. Most of all, they had to serve the special needs of men living a prolonged bachelor existence. They had to provide male companionship when that was desired. They also had to satisfy the frequent urge for female companionship, especially among those men for whom masturbation and homosexuality were neither adequate nor desirable forms of sexual gratification. Fulfilling these needs were saloons, billiard halls, and brothels.

There were between five and six hundred saloons in Detroit during the 1850s and 1860s. The saloon was more than just a place to buy a drink. There were, of course, the many roles the pub played in working-class neighborhoods. Downtown, the saloon might double as a boarding house, a dance hall, or a brothel. Mostly it was a men's club, an extension of other bachelor activities. A "veteran beer seller" described a typical Sunday in his saloon: "Young men comes in and sets around the table talking for an hour yet, and drink only one glass apiece. They don't seem to want much peer [sic], but they got no other place to go, all the while. Maybe their boarding places is not pleasant, or so, and so they come in here shust to pass away the time, young men that go to church part of the time, too."[12]

The billiard hall provided bachelors and other males with a similar environment, although in these years it was of lesser importance and was not as suggestive of evil and immorality to order-minded citizens in Detroit as other downtown amusements would quickly become. Pocket billiards was a competitive game all could play at relatively little expense, while the room itself became a rendezvous and social center. Billiards enjoyed a sudden burst of popularity in the United States during the 1850s. The first national billiard periodical appeared in 1856, and three years later the widely read *Frank Leslie's Illustrated Newspaper* began a regular column on billiards. No longer were the devotees of the sport just the leisurely elite. They now began to include the working class, with German and Irish championship players joining the traditional Anglo-Saxons. Billiards caught on in Detroit as it did everywhere. In fact, what approximated the first national championship match was played in Detroit in 1859 between a New York Irishman and a local German. It generated enormous interest in the city, and gave added impetus to the game's already growing popularity. By the mid–1860s, just the local demand was enough to sustain a Detroit company that manufactured billiard tables. Billiard halls sprang up in the city beginning about 1850. By 1862, there were a dozen listed in the city directory, but probably twice that many really existed.[13]

The house of prostitution, however, was the most important and colorful of the urban amusements enjoyed by the transient and unattached male population. Men in the nineteenth century, more so than today it would appear, visited prostitutes not as an occasional dalliance but as a way of maintaining their bachelorhood. Paul Jacobson has shown that during the second half of the nineteenth century the age at which American males married rose steadily. Available Michigan data support this conclusion. In 1871–75, 56 percent of the state's marriages involved men over the age of twenty-four. By 1896–1900, it was up to 61 percent.[14] The popularity of the brothel grew in tandem with transiency and extended bachelorhood among males, reaching its peak in the late nineteenth century. Already by 1850, however, it had become more visible on the urban landscape than ever before. Ironically, prostitution grew apace with the "cult of true womanhood" and its Victorian emphasis on sexual purity and innocence. Since men, on the other hand, were still allowed their sexual escapades, a subclass of women was required to serve them. So the whore became more legitimate at the same time she became more disreputable as a female. Brothels in Detroit, as we have already seen, were quite numerous and conspicuous by the 1850s, and increasingly controversial. It is difficult to determine exactly how many there were. One local editor claimed in 1850 that there were over one hundred, but the compiler of the city directory reported only thirty-one two years later.[15] One thing is clear, however. Brothels were proliferating, especially by the early 1860s when Detroit came out of the economic doldrums of the previous years and when it served as a way station for Michigan troops during the Civil War.

Map II–2 plots the locations of Detroit's saloons, billiard halls, and brothels in the mid–1860s.[16] It shows that they were found primarily in and around the downtown, where the many unattached transient males they served tended to live, a segment of the population to which such places (brothels especially) would certainly not be as obnoxious as they were to the working-class families in the outer residential neighborhoods. The symbiotic relationship between these amusements and elements of the population downtown is amply illustrated by

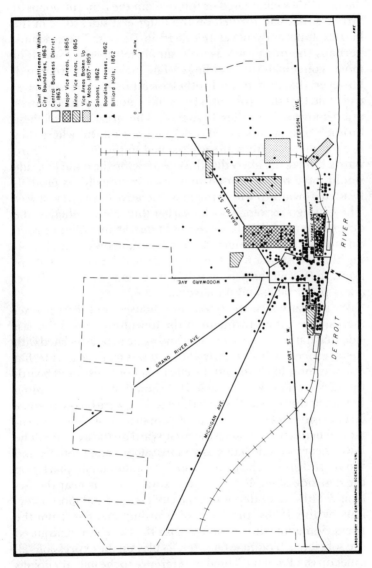

MAP II–2: Boarding Houses, Saloons, Billiard Halls, and Vice Areas, 1862.

the evolution of the spatial patterns of vice. When the mobs of the late 1850s eliminated or thinned out the concentrations of brothels that had formed on the outer east side, some of the houses apparently never relocated in Detroit. The madams, perhaps the prostitutes as well, simply left town in search of more congenial surroundings. The newspapers reported, however, that most of the brothels continued to operate in Detroit, and that the prostitutes from those not able to begin anew often moved into other bordellos. The great bulk of these brothels, the papers noted, relocated downtown, where they swelled the vice areas already formed in the First and Third wards.[17] It is even likely that the vice areas on the outer east side would have broken up on their own eventually, as brothels headed downtown where the most lucrative environment was. The Chicago sociologists who earlier this century plugged the development of the classic red-light district into their ecological interpretative framework were undoubtedly correct in stating that prostitution in the long run had limited spatial options. In Detroit the process was helped along by mob violence, a less predictable and impersonal force.[18]

While transients, their boarding houses, and their amusements were found throughout the downtown, it was the east side that harbored most of them and came to be associated with them, especially by the early 1860s. It was on the east side that one was most likely to find the cheapest flophouses and boarding saloons. The data in Table II–1 show that regular boarding houses in the Third Ward on the east side were on the average larger and sheltered a greater proportion of young, unattached males than those in the First Ward on the west side. The lower near east side had many more saloons and brothels, and the most disreputables ones, too. The amusement quarter on the east side along Franklin and Atwater streets near the Detroit & Milwaukee depot was the city's largest and most notorious by the 1860s, the focus of growing attention from the press. Sometime during or just after the Civil War, it acquired the sobriquet "Potomac Quarter," a play on the expression "all quiet on the Potomac," used in reference to the military doings in Virginia.[19]

That the lower near east side, from Gratiot to the river, developed so fully as an area of saloons, dance halls, and brothels is not surprising. Prostitution there dated back to the 1830s. Legitimate business expanded from the city center eastward only along Jefferson Avenue, which became an oasis of opulence in a generally deprived area. Many of the buildings to the east of the business district were in poor repair, and attractive as living space primarily to those who could afford nothing better. Thus the area had long been the home of some of Detroit's poorest people, particularly blacks and lower-class French. In short, it had developed into what the sociologist Gerald Suttles would call a "defeated neighborhood," a part of the city harboring the least powerful elements of the population, and one most likely to attract the kind of people and institutions that are antithetical to the interests of more influential or self-conscious family residential neighborhoods.[20] Thus, while almost every street on the lower near east side had its share of boarding houses, saloons, and brothels, these places were much more circumscribed on the lower west side, where nearby residential neighborhoods were quite influential indeed.

FASHIONABLE RESIDENTIAL NEIGHBORHOODS

The streets that boarding houses and low amusements could not penetrate on the near west side belonged to Detroit's most successful, wealthy, and prominent citizens—merchants, manufacturers, bankers, and lawyers. Fashionable residential areas, it might be recalled, had begun to form as far back as the 1830s. Over the next twenty-five years they expanded considerably. Few prominent Detroiters lived outside these areas. With the exception of the wealthy strip along Jefferson Avenue on the east side, the fashionable neighborhoods lay to the immediate northwest of the central business district.[21] Like other urban elites in the mid-nineteenth century, Detroit's wealthy residents lived near the heart of the city. It was traditionally prestigious space, and they could be close to their businesses, offices, or real estate. Greater than the convenience was their proprietory attitude about the downtown. They owned it and profited from it, so they should oversee it as well. Although the fashionable neighborhoods were not self-contained—there were few shops and stores mixed in with the homes—and although the elite obviously felt none of the insecurity and frustration that helped to forge neighborhood spirit in the immigrant, working-class areas, wealthy and prominent citizens were as spatially self-conscious as any group in the city. They consistently sought out residential locations among people of similar status—neighborhoods that would provide them with an attractive environment and would clearly set them apart from the lower orders. The fashionable urban enclave was a way for the elite to define itself in a society lacking the trappings of a nobility.[22]

If there had been higher ground in Detroit, like Beacon Hill in Boston, for instance, the elite would have been drawn to it to sit magisterially above the masses. As it was, Detroit's wealthy citizens satisfied their spatial needs by laying out and improving their own well-marked residential neighborhoods in the high-priced tracts of land bounded by Shelby, Larned, and Fifth streets, and Michigan Avenue, much of which had originally belonged to Lewis Cass, prominent Detroiter and presidential candidate in 1848. By the 1850s, many fashionable citizens had left behind their old town houses, which were being crowded out by the expansion of the business district, and were moving into countrified mansions built to the popular Gothic and Italianate designs. These stylish villas rose one after another on the spacious lots along Fort, Congress, and Lafayette streets on the west side, but still not far at all from the center of the city. Fort Street West, in particular, became the Broadway of Detroit. Residents along its most elegant stretch, from Griswold to Fifth, formed a "Street Committee" in 1856. Its members were all prominent citizens and included John Owen, one of Detroit's wealthiest men. The committee was to supervise the paving of Fort Street and the placement of meandering sidewalks, to be flanked by maples and elms, carefully planted to provide a graceful canopy over the whole. Tastefully designed gas lamps were to be the final touch.[23]

It was through their churches, however, that Detroit's well-to-do gave best expression to their desire for a spatial identity. Between 1852 and 1861, wealthy citizens commissioned some of the best local architects to design four splendid new churches. In fact, St. John's Episcopal Church at the corner of Woodward Avenue and High Street was built almost entirely with funds donated by Henry P. Baldwin, a successful shoe manufacturer. The most impressive of the new churches was the Fort Street Presbyterian. Completed in 1855, it was described by an ecstatic *Free Press* as "one of the best specimens of church architecture to be met in any city of the West, and we may almost say, of the East." Located in the heart of the fashionable west side at Fort and Third, its first list of pew-holders read like a Who's Who of Detroit. With its two-hundred-and thirty-foot Gothic spire rising majestically above the city, the church established elite space better than any other Detroit landmark.[24]

The growing sense of group identity and group interest displayed by the elite in the development of the fashionable residential neighborhoods during the 1850s was especially evident in the organization of the Detroit Board of Trade. The idea of a mercantile organization and exchange was one that dated back to the 1830s, but it made little headway through the 1840s. Toward the end of that decade, and into the 1850s, the newspapers exhorted the city's businessmen to form a Board of Trade. "Association is the great modern lever," wrote the *Advertiser* in 1847. "No large project is carried forward now without associated effort. . . ." In 1849, the *Advertiser* called for the construction of a Merchants' Exchange. "Why should Detroit remain behind her neighbors," it asked.[25] Silas Farmer, Detroit's superb nineteenth-century historian, attributes the tardiness of Detroit in establishing a permanent mercantile organization to the keen competition among the city's businessmen. It was of no little consequence, moreover, that the entrepreneurial class throughout these years had the reputation for being a lackadaisical and unimaginative group that moved too cautiously in investing on behalf of the city's economic progress.[26] In the 1850s the business community turned over a new leaf, and in 1856 it finally established a permanent Board of Trade. From the outset, this organization clearly had much wider support from the mercantile class than any of its short-lived predecessors, and it grew rapidly. By the early 1860s it was made up of some of Detroit's most important commercial interests, including wholesale and forwarding merchants, grain dealers, and shippers.[27]

The residential patterns of the members of the Board of

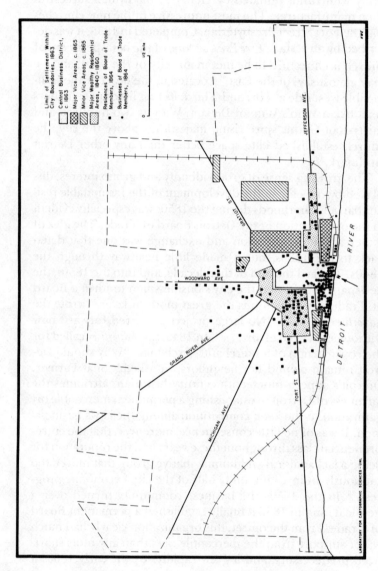

MAP II-3: Residences and Businesses of Board of Trade Members, 1864.

Trade are useful in substantiating the existence of a spatial exclusivity among the city's elite. Map II–3 reveals that in 1864 the men who belonged to this organization lived and worked in those parts of the city traditionally used by the city's wealthy and prominent citizens.[28] Most lived downtown, close to their businesses. The rest were bunched together in the fashionable areas north of the business district that were just beginning to emerge by the mid–1860s. As much as any institution in the city, the Board of Trade represented Detroit's men of property and standing, and their distinct spatial perspective. This perspective had as its focus those things that symbolized and outlined the city's elite space: the impressive brick facades along Woodward and Jefferson avenues, the massive complex of the Michigan Central Railroad, the bustling warehouse district, and the mansions of Fort Street West and other fashionable residential areas. Yet also not far out of focus were the streets and alleyways given over to the transient population and its amusements. The homes of some of Detroit's richest men along Congress Street West or Jefferson Avenue, for example, were but a long stone's throw from cheap bordellos and saloon flophouses. From the vantage point of today's sprawling metropolis, with its vast distances isolating various urban groups and activities, this was an extraordinary urban environment.

How conspicuous the transient, low-amusement areas were to the men of property and standing living and working downtown would also depend on prevailing bourgeois attitudes about the life styles and activities associated with such areas. Historians have recently pointed to the growing feeling among middle-class reformers in the mid-nineteenth century that real meaning and satisfaction in life came chiefly from home and family. Domesticity was both a retreat from chaotic society and a laboratory for the perfection of the individual. Single-family houses set apart on roomy lots and fashioned in the new rustic, romantic architectural styles gave ultimate expression to this ideal—visual statements of the stability and integrity of their owners at a time of social restlessness and moral decay.[29] We now know that while all types of Americans were footloose in the nineteenth century the propertied classes and the well-to-do moved about less often than the lower classes. The transiency of others worried those to whom it logically appeared to be the product of irresponsibility and lack of industriousness. What was an accepted pattern of living for many Americans, particularly young unmarried males, was to men of property and standing in any given community a sign of personal failure. The *Free Press* gave a subtle hint of this, as well as of the bourgeois faith in the stable domesticity of the single-family house, when in 1867 it contemplated the disturbing prospect that eastern-style working-class tenements might begin to sprout up in Detroit as more and more people flowed into the city. The paper assured its readers, however, that this would not happen, and that the city's working classes would continue to enjoy the blessings of single-family dwellings. "He who owns the roof that covers him and his," it added, "is a much better citizen, a better Christian, and a happier man."[30] Michael Katz has suggested that it was these feelings that encouraged the well-to-do in mid-nineteenth-century Hamilton, Ontario, to take in boarders, particularly young males. By so doing they could provide these young men with an idealized home environment. The boarders would be supervised as they passed through the crucial period of drifting and "semi-autonomy" between the end of parental control and the onset of married life.[31]

We might hypothesize, then, that the respectable classes in Detroit found little to like about the boarding-house areas downtown. Indeed, they may have viewed the worst of these areas, such as the tough riverfront sections, much as urbanites today view skid rows, which, after all, are but putrefied remnants of the nineteenth-century transient subculture. That is, these areas were stigmatized, their habitués considered beyond the pale of social normality and degenerated to a potentially dangerous, unpredictable state of random action. One is reminded of the way moralizing sociologists in the early twentieth century characterized the people in rooming houses as "spiritual nomads."[32]

The brothels and bars patronized by the floating population, especially its lower-class elements, seemed as destined for reprobation as the cheap boarding houses. The new ideal of domesticity, Clifford Clark, Jr., argues, made the home the proper arena of entertainment as well. The house plans laid out by reform-minded architects clearly separated the family's rooms from those in which guests were welcome. While this was meant to reinforce the private side of family life, it was also intended to encourage domestic socializing, for the front parlor now emerged as the home's "public" space, in which a more controlled and correct form of entertainment was to be enjoyed than that which often took place in the promiscuous city. As the front parlor gained favor, the old public house and the streetcorner fell into disrepute.[33]

It was a growing distaste for their *public* quality that as much as anything made saloons and beer halls (to say nothing of the brothels) offensive to reformers. As elsewhere in urban America in the nineteenth century, clergymen and other prominent citizens among the native-born Protestant population generally took the lead in Detroit in establishing temperance and sabbatarian movements. Proponents of a new Sunday liquor law in 1860–61, for example, included George Duffield, Detroit's most eminent Presbyterian minister, and Eber Ward, shipper, capitalist, and one of the city's richest men. The standards of public propriety among reformers such as these were high indeed. The *Advertiser,* a paper sympathetic to the sabbatarian cause, was so strict in setting its standards of decorous behavior on the Lord's Day that it seemed outraged one Sunday in 1854 when a group of men was heard laughing out loud on a streetcorner. If it was wrong to imbibe on the Sabbath, it was certainly worse to do so in a public manner. The sight and sound of people amusing themselves, not just the pastimes, were offensive to reformers. The sabbatarians wanted the saloons closed completely, but even those who felt that that went too far shared some of the sabbatarians' sensitivity to public displays. When reformers renewed their attacks on Detroit's saloons and beer halls in the 1860s it was conceded all around that these places ought to be discreet. Thus a compromise municipal ordinance in 1866 allowed saloons to open on Sunday, but with no signs, no music, and no dancing.[34]

The respectable classes in Detroit, therefore, if our hypothesis is correct, naturally cast a distrustful eye on the transient, low-amusement areas that grew up all around them downtown during the late 1850s and early 1860s. That even the many lower-class transients and unattached males who dominated the population living in and frequenting these areas had legitimate social needs was a point lost on those prejudiced by the standards of middle-class respectability. This prejudice helped to cast the Potomac Quarter and similar, if less notorious, areas in bolder relief and to focus attention upon them. One thing is clear. If Detroit's men of property and standing were to see any evidence that they had something to fear from these areas, that they were in fact not merely disreputable but also dangerous, then the reaction would be swift. This is precisely what happened. The focus of the elite on the transient, low-amusement areas was above all the product of a crisis downtown in crime and disorder.

THREE
The Crisis Downtown

Law and order became an important issue among many of Detroit's leading citizens during the 1850s and early 1860s. Any complex society, like Detroit's, would have difficulty in achieving a consensus about what constituted deviant behavior. An act considered criminal or disorderly by one group might have been tolerated as quite normal by another. A fist-fight outside a saloon, a collection of noisy young men on a streetcorner, or a case of petty larceny were likely to be more offensive to wealthy residents living in fashionable neighborhoods than to transient workers living in tough riverfront areas. If Detroit's elite residents were by nature less restrained in defining criminal and disorderly behavior, their concern was no abstraction. For one thing, they were being victimized by criminals and ruffians. While they viewed the German brothel riots, for example, as little more than curious and colorful expressions of neighborhood outrage, only mildly disruptive of the city's good order, disturbances downtown were an entirely different matter. Crime and disorder interacted with the dramatic spatial developments in the heart of the city, particularly the formation of rowdy low-amusement quarters, to forge changing attitudes toward policing and to lead ultimately to the organization of a professional police force in 1865.

In reorganizing its police, Detroit did what every other major American city and many secondary ones did between 1840 and 1870. Historians have only in the past ten or fifteen years shown an interest in the subject of nineteenth-century police

53

reform. The first studies were legal and administrative in their focus, confined mostly to narrative descriptions of the step-by-step demise of the old constabulary and the steady, but often controversial evolution of the professionals. Scholars seemed preoccupied with the politics of police reform. Its causes, on the other hand, were considered only in cursory fashion, more often assumed than proved. Cities, it would seem, moved inevitably toward modern policing as a consequence of soaring levels of crime and disorder in an era of phenomenal growth and profound social change.[1]

There is now some question, however, about how unprecedented the levels of mid-century crime and disorder really were, and about their relationship to police reform. Philadelphians, after all, were complaining about troublesome elements in their city a full generation before the advent of reformism. Moreover, many of the urban mobs of the 1830s and after defended the status quo and were supported by the respectable classes.[2] Consequently, historians have become more interested than before in the perceptions of police reformers about the law-and-order problem. It is important, they say, to look closely at what drove reformers to promote such radical institutional departures, rather than to assume that this was a natural response to crime waves and mobs.

In trying to penetrate the minds of police reformers, these scholars have worked under a handicap. Important and influential urbanites were not in the habit of writing down their thoughts about local governmental and political matters, in contrast to state and national leaders, who, removed from their constituencies, often left a wealth of political correspondence behind for the historian to peruse. Local politicians and men of influence spoke to each other and to interested citizens across restaurant tables, office desks, or store counters, and in dining rooms and front parlors. Nonetheless, whatever the limitations of the evidence, it would appear from the most recent scholarship that order-minded urbanites and police reformers were worried above all about the prospect of a "dangerous class" overtaking their cities. These fears were more intense than similar concerns among urbanites in earlier periods because of the powerful current of social and economic change that flowed through the mid-nineteenth-century city. The elements the respectable classes feared most seemed to vary from city to city. They might have been Irish immigrants, lower-class workers, vagrants and tramps, or poor people in general. The order-minded might have seen in the dangerous class a real increase in crime and disorder, or they might just have been concerned about a segment of the population whose values and behavior were suspect by definition. But the professional police was created and employed by the dominant classes in an atmosphere of crisis to control subordinate groups in the social and economic structure.[3]

There are a number of questions, then, that we need to answer about police reform in Detroit. What was the real role played by crime and disorder? Who exactly promoted police reform? Was there a "dangerous class"? Who comprised it? Why was a professional police seen as the most appropriate response to conditions? We need to ask these questions with an eye to the indigenous qualities of the city that gave meaning to the problem of law and order. In short, we need to subordinate police history to urban history, and in particular, to one of the city's most essential features—its spatial arrangements. What was it about the *environment* of mid-nineteenth-century Detroit that was likely to make certain residents more concerned than ever before about law and order, and also to make the new professional police idea such an attractive solution to the problem?

CRIME AND ITS VICTIMS

In the 1830s and 1840s, the only crimes that took place with any regularity in Detroit were burglary and arson. During 1834, in fact, the city experienced something of a crime wave. "Lurking vagabonds hang around us like blackbirds about a cornfield," one newspaper commented. A number of prominent citizens, including the then mayor and three of his predecessors, responded by forming a "Society for the Suppression of Felony." This vigilante organization had a standing posse of twenty men who would round up criminals and return stolen property for members of the society, or anyone willing to cover costs. Crime waves like that of 1834, however, were quite rare, and Detroiters could write off most crime, which usually came in short spurts, as the work of another "gang of rascals" who happened to be in town. Much of the time people seemed unconcerned about crime.[4]

Beginning in the late 1840s, however, an abrupt change took place in the perception of the city's crime problem among residents. During the early 1850s, a grand jury reported on the persistence of violent street crime, the newspapers warned their readers that a wave of muggings or even a murder could no longer be considered an aberration, and the city's police justice complained that many residents were afraid to walk the streets at night and that shopkeepers half expected each morning to find that their stores had been broken into. By 1863, city officials could assert baldly that "almost every crime in the catalogue of crimes" was being committed daily in the streets of Detroit.[5]

Was serious crime really increasing by the 1850s? Newspaper reports offer a clue, for even if local editors were simply responding to public concern about crime when they offered readers impressionistic descriptions of the law-and-order "problem," they still had to produce the evidence in the form of actual criminal incidents. These seemed to present themselves in growing abundance. Between 1848 and 1853, the *Free Press* could report only four city murders, crimes not likely to be ignored by journalists regardless of their preoccupation with law and order. In the shorter period from 1854 to 1858, the paper reported thirteen murders in the city, an increase from the earlier years that surpassed even the rate of population growth.[6] There were, it would seem, more crimes of all kinds to report on a day-to-day basis in the 1850s and early 1860s. A wave of crime the newspapers documented in 1854 was like nothing the city had ever known before. The *Advertiser* counted ten muggings in one week. In 1855, a rash of burglaries plagued the city. "They have of late become so frequent in the city," the *Free Press* charged, "that we are totally unable to keep pace with them."[7]

Jail commitments and police court arraignments, the extant data on which are presented in Table III-1, seem to confirm

TABLE III-1:   COUNTY JAIL COMMITMENTS AND POLICE COURT
ARRAIGNMENTS FOR CRIMES OF THEFT AND
PERSONAL VIOLENCE, 1847–64
(PER THOUSAND CAPITA)

		Theft[a]	Violence[b]
Wayne County Jail, Commitments:	1847–48	5.4	5.0
	1853–54	7.2	5.5
	1863–64	8.3	6.8
Detroit Police Court, Arraignments:	1854–55	6.8	11.1
	1855–56	4.9	8.9
	1856–57	4.9	8.2
	1857–58	5.7	13.4
	1862–63	6.5	12.9
	1863–64	6.5	13.0

[a]Burglary, larceny, robbery, horsetheft, breaking and entering.
[b]Murder, manslaughter, assault, assault and battery, rape.
SOURCE : *Free Press*, November 18, 1847, May 16, 1848, May 27, November 16, 1854, July 6, 1855, July 11, 1856, July 4, 1857, July 2, 1858, January 6, April 15, July 4, October 8, November 2, December 1, 1863, January 1, 7, February 2, March 3, April 1, 4, May 2, June 1, July 1, 6, August 1, September 1, October 2, 16, 1864.

both the crime wave of 1854–55 and the generally rising crime rate between the late 1840s and early 1860s. (The Wayne County Jail, located in Detroit, was mainly a city jail. The Police Court was the regular criminal court of Detroit, before which all felony cases were initially examined.) These statistics admittedly have limited value. Data on "assaults" may say more about the amount of family quarrels and barroom fights among drinking companions than they say about violent street crime; and in any case the statistics reflect the diligence and efficiency of the deputies in making arrests. In the absence of any better data, however, we must consider these to be at least broad indicators of rising levels of the kind of criminal behavior that the press and others in Detroit were concerned about.

That crime may have been increasing is significant. That it was taking place downtown, however, is more important. There it posed a threat to the city's respectable classes, who in 1850 were made nervously aware of how much their entrepreneurial successes made them particularly vulnerable to the depredations of the underclass. In November of that year, saboteurs acting on behalf of mid-state farmers angry with railroad abuses set fire to the new Michigan Central freight depot. The building was a total loss and had to be rebuilt from the bottom up. The indicated arsonists were tried in Detroit in the spring and summer of 1851 amid rumors of further sabotage. The city's business community was both outraged and on edge, and no doubt shared the sentiments of the fashionable lawyer, James A. Van Dyke, who had successfully defended the Gratiot Street rioters of 1849, but who now was retained by the Michigan Central. He bemoaned the efforts of radicals "to reduce our young and beautous (sic) city, to a mass of black and smoldering ashes, and to entomb in its ruins, properties that were the reward of long and ceaseless toil." Detroit's mayor, the promising young wholesale merchant, Zachariah Chandler, responded to his colleagues', as well as his own, trepidation by increasing the fire watch and enlisting special policemen to guard important downtown properties.[8]

The general crime that plagued the downtown in these years occurred even on the major thoroughfares. Detroit's "best citizens" were often victimized. To cite just a few examples, burglars broke into the property of railroad magnate James F. Joy in 1850, one of Eber Ward's warehouses in 1854, the residence of Mayor Christian H. Buhl in 1860, and the homes of two fashionable lawyers, D. B. Duffield and C. I. Walker, in 1864. The *Free Press* complained in 1864 about the many robberies taking place on the busiest downtown streets. The *Advertiser and Tribune* reported soon thereafter that "gentlemen" had taken to wearing revolvers.[9] The only sources available for determining where crime was taking place during the 1850s and early 1860s are the newspapers. Map III–1 is a plotting of all the crimes of theft and personal violence reported in the *Free Press* in 1854 and 1864 for which precise locations were given. The *Free Press* was Detroit's most widely read daily, and it prob-

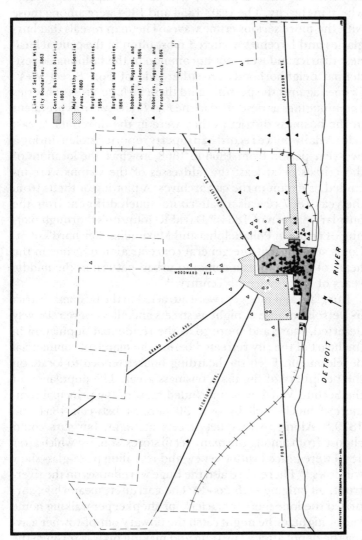

MAP III-1: Crime Patterns, 1854, 1864.

Limit of Settlement Within
City Boundaries, 1863

Central Business District,
c. 1863

Major Wealthy Residential
Areas, 1860

○ Burglaries and Larcenies,
1854

△ Burglaries and Larcenies,
1864

● Robberies, Muggings, and
Personal Violence, 1854

▲ Robberies, Muggings, and
Personal Violence, 1864

ably tried as much as possible to report on happenings everywhere in the city. The years 1854 and 1864 were among those with the more serious crime waves. The map reveals that burglaries and larcenies occurred most often in the central business district and were not uncommon in the fashionable residential neighborhoods on either side of Fort Street West. Crimes against the person—and these include street robberies and muggings as described in the *Free Press*—were as prevalent in the business district as they were in the disreputable east side. A daily police record of property reported stolen during a two-year period from 1866 to 1868, in which the locations of the crimes or at least the addresses of the victims were included, is extant in the city archives. A plotting of thefts from the year 1867 reveals a pattern not much different from the burglary pattern of 1864.[10] David R. Johnson's thorough plotting of crime in Philadelphia and Maximilian Reichard's of St. Louis suggest that the general concentration of crime in the heart of the city was a common urban pattern in the middle years of the nineteenth century.[11]

Burglars and muggers were attracted to the business district in Detroit because at night its streets and alleys were relatively deserted, more and more so as the residential population in the heart of the city retreated before the march of commercial development. Even the boarding houses tended to locate on the periphery of the main business areas. The population of the Second Ward, which included most of the principal commercial blocks, fell by over 30 percent between 1854 and 1870.[12] Along these quiet streets at night, burglars could choose from among the many retail stores, some of which after 1849 were graced with the new and revealing plate-glass show windows.[13] There were also the huge warehouses on the riverfront, all bulging with goods. The garrotter, meanwhile, surprised the lone merchant, clerk, or shopkeeper walking home late at night, or he might catch the unwary out-of-towner leaving the depot after a late train and making his way through the unfamiliar streets in search of a hotel, a tavern, or perhaps a brothel. Detroit's waterfront became a nighttime no man's land, where the "almost daily disturbance of the public peace as well as assaults and robberies of individuals" prompted the Common Council to order an investigation in 1863.[14]

The crime waves of the 1850s were bothersome enough to ignite the first serious talk about establishing a regular, professional police force in Detroit. (A letter to the *Free Press* in 1849 from an unidentifiable person had called for Detroit to adopt a full-scale "preventive police" on the London–New York model, but the idea generated absolutely no interest.)[15] When the city exploded in crime in the summer of 1854, the Common Council drew up an estimate on the cost of maintaining a regular night watch. Any expenditures would have to be approved by a public meeting of taxpayers. The council decided to act, according to one official, because of pressure from prominent citizens and some of the newspapers. Certainly the Whig-Republican *Advertiser* supported police reform. The Democratic *Free Press* was dead set against it, however, and rejoiced when the public meeting voted the proposal down.[16] Later that year, the continuing crime problem, particularly burglaries in the central business district, made even the *Free Press* come out in support of some sort of regular night watch. In the meantime, the city's young police justice, B. Rush Bagg, traveled east at the request of "prominent citizens" to study several city police systems in that part of the country. Bagg returned convinced that Detroit should organize a professional police force, and he wrote a series of public letters to the newspapers outlining his position and presenting detailed proposals. For over a year Bagg lobbied for the adoption of a professional system and early in 1856 finally succeeded in getting the Common Council to call another citizens' meeting. Again, the taxpayers voted the question down, and this time both of the principal dailies agreed with the public's decision not to make the commitment to full-time police.[17]

Police reform failed in the mid–1850s for two reasons. First, there was the inevitable concern about higher taxes that would be needed to pay for a system whose annual cost was variously estimated at from fifteen to thirty-three thousand dollars. Detroit's economic slide, which began in 1854, had become critical by 1856, and the city was in no mood to spend unnecessarily. "Retrenchment is more desireable than extravagance in these close times," the *Free Press* advised in 1856.[18] Second, and more important, downtown businessmen were not yet ready to commit themselves to a regular city police force, despite the fact that criminals often victimized them. The citizens' meetings that so swiftly brushed aside efforts at police reform were assemblies traditionally dominated by "the larger property owners," according to Silas Farmer. The *Free Press* based its opposition to police reorganization on the fact that businessmen and respectable citizens had no confidence in it. Part of the problem clearly was the question of police distribution. Everyone seemed to assume that since this would be a municipal agency, publicly funded, some effort would have to be made to spread the policemen around the city, perhaps with an emphasis on the more populous or the largest wards. Yet to downtown interests this made little tactical sense in the battle against crime.[19]

What businessmen and other prominent property owners in the heart of the city preferred to do about the crime problem at this stage was to take care of it themselves through their own devices. This, of course, they had always done, for the most part. Many hired private watchmen to guard their offices, stores, or warehouses. It was also common for shopkeepers to let clerks or other employees have sleeping rooms on the premises so that they might deter burglars. With the mounting crime rates of the 1850s and the obstacles blocking the establishment of an efficient city police that would serve its special needs, the business community moved gradually toward adapting the preventive, professional police idea to the requirements of privatism and self-interest. Late in 1854, local insurance companies, which were understandably annoyed by that year's rash of burglaries and suspected incendiary fires and which in the past had often posted rewards for the apprehension of criminals, organized a paid night watch of twenty-two men to patrol the central business district. "What the city has neglected to establish," wrote the *Free Press,* which in late 1854 briefly supported police reform, "has at last been established by private enterprise." The *Advertiser* was no doubt glancing at the insurance police as a model when shortly thereafter it advocated a general city police paid for by private contributions. The insurance police force itself was short-lived, and the idea of mercenary preventive policing did not take hold immediately, but it was not dead.[20]

In late 1857, the problem of burglaries and muggings in the business district became serious enough for the Common Council to designate a room at City Hall, in the "most convenient and central portion of the city" (in the words of the *Free Press*) where a few of the deputies would be available all night long.[21] They would still not be patrolling the business district on a regular basis, however. In the spring of 1858, the *Advertiser* reported that a "decided feeling" existed among downtown businessmen that some sort of new action was needed to fight crime. On that very same day the *Free Press* suggested that Detroit's merchants and shopkeepers follow the lead of their colleagues in other cities (including some that had regular night watches) and organize a private patrol paid for by individual subscriptions. Two local detectives immediately offered their services, but there is no evidence that they ever set up a patrol. Eight months later, however, the dailies were pleased to report that the man responsible for Chicago's excellent Merchants' Police had arrived in the city and at the request of local businessmen was in the process of organizing a similar force for Detroit. No sooner was it in operation than two sheriff's deputies established another, but smaller, patrol just for the warehouse district on the west side.[22]

Expensive as these private systems undoubtedly were for those who subscribed to them, they offered obvious advantages. The *Free Press*, which was delighted to see the crime problem dealt with without recourse to public spending, noted that a "public police would cost less to individuals, but would be far less serviceable, as no attention is paid to particular private interests under such a system." In other words, a municipal police force would be under certain pressures to serve a variety of interests, and the downtown business community would not get the special protection it needed.[23] The mercenary police forces also were seen as an improvement over the deputies and constables because they patrolled the streets and alleys, working to prevent criminals from acting in the first place. The policemen walked predetermined beats in the business district, making special efforts to see that clerks and janitors had not carelessly left doors and windows open, a major inducement, it was felt, to criminals. There is no evidence on the numerical strength of these police forces, nor on how many businessmen subscribed to them. The patrolmen, in any case, guarded all the properties on their beats and apprehended criminals regardless of where the crime took place. Organizers and proponents, however, hoped that businessmen not subscribing would eventually be shamed into signing up and sharing costs. The Merchants' Police set up by the Chicagoan operated in Detroit for a year, when it was taken over by a local group and renamed the Merchants' and Business Men's Police. From that point on there are no further references to it in the press.[24]

Thus Detroit may have continued to function without regular city police, but the crime waves of the 1850s and the vulnerability of important downtown interests had generated a new approach toward crime. The preventive, professional concept now had a foothold. The business police forces answered a real need and apparently were effective, at least to the extent that a few burglars, so the *Free Press* contended, were driven away from the more heavily patrolled areas to the less well-patrolled ones.[25] The debate over any kind of city police would henceforth have to concern itself with the question of how serviceable such a force would be to the downtown interests that had come to expect more thoroughgoing police protection than the municipality traditionally had provided or could be expected to provide.

THE PROBLEM OF DISORDER

Had the concern about law and order downtown been limited to burglaries and robberies, private police measures might have satisfied most of the city's businessmen for some time. By the early 1860s, however, there were many Detroiters who thought their city was suffering from a serious malaise, whose symptoms were ruffianism and disorder—from major riots to the problem of streetcorner loungers and rowdy places of amusement—and whose cure required a dose of more extensive and formalized police procedures than ever before contemplated, by public officials *or* private interests.

Citizens worried about the problem of street disturbances needed only to look at what had happened to the venerable fire companies. By the mid–1850s the volunteers had lost the reputation for orderliness they had sustained for thirty years. To be sure, they were still not brawling gangs. Full lists of firemen are not available, but there is no indication that the men were of a lesser breed, even if the city's fashionable young men were not as likely to join anymore. The officers of each company listed in the city directory of 1857 were mostly a scattering of shopkeepers, craftsmen, and office workers. In the meantime, the systematic positioning of many of the fire stations along Larned Street, from Wayne Street on the west side to Riopelle on the east, made it less likely they would strike a natural neighborhood vein. Only Company No. 10, whose station was located in the middle of Corktown, seemed to have a clear ethnic character. Most of its officers had Irish names. If, however, there were as yet no pitched battles between companies, it was quite evident to many residents that the volunteers were not what they used to be. There was a lot more rowdiness around the station houses. The men hollered and chanted as they ran to and from fires. In 1855, the city had to order the companies to stop the annoying and dangerous practice of running their apparatus on downtown sidewalks. A number of the volunteers retaliated by resigning, then harassing their replacements at fires. The disorderliness of the volunteers began to take its toll on the traditional attitude toward the fire companies. By 1860, the Common Council was purchasing steam fire engines, which made fire-fighting less competitive than when done with the old hand pumps, while also requiring that apparatus be pulled by horses, not gangs of men. The *Free Press* reported that the intention of officials was to do away with the volunteer system entirely because of its disorderliness. The paper was disappointed with the companies for showing signs of behaving like the Philadelphia and Baltimore outfits with which they had been contrasted so often in the past. In 1861, in a move that anticipated developments soon to transpire in po-

licing, the volunteer firemen gave way to full-time professionals.[26]
The problem of street disorder in downtown Detroit, however, went far beyond the volunteer firemen. At the heart of
the matter was the proliferation of saloons, dance halls, and
brothels in areas around the business district and some of the
fashionable residential streets, especially after 1857. First,
there were the houses of ill fame chased away by the mobs on
the outer east side. Many of them scrambled for space downtown, and "aristocratic and select communities" were sometimes surprised to find these places suddenly in their midst. In
one instance, a building on Jefferson Avenue that had only recently been a church was converted into a dance hall.[27] There
had always been houses of prostitution downtown, but the majority of these newer places were cheap and rowdy. The informal separation of high-class and low-class vice had broken
down. These trends continued in the early 1860s. Renewed
city growth meant more downtown boarding houses, which in
turn spawned more saloons and brothels. In the meantime,
Detroit served as a way station for Michigan troops during the
Civil War. Barracks for ten thousand men were erected on the
city's eastern fringe. Boisterous soldiers now often flooded
downtown amusement areas, and the new business encouraged even more saloons and brothels to open up.[28]
For the prominent and influential people who did their business downtown and lived nearby, the spread of these low
amusements was quite disturbing. It began to show noticeably
by the summer of 1858. A letter to the *Free Press* complained
about the growing numbers of drunks and rowdies who were
now often to be found loitering on Woodbridge Avenue downtown, where they pestered businessmen and other passers-by.
The *Free Press* itself noted with disgust a few weeks later that
dance halls had sprung up in the very heart of the city near
businesses and churches. A local judge added his voice to the
chorus, pointing to the dance halls that existed on Jefferson
Avenue near Beaubien Street, places the *Free Press* claimed
were particularly offensive to "the ladies" and others on that
fashionable thoroughfare. "Respectable" residents of the First
Ward complained in 1860 about at least one house of ill fame

near their neighborhood. The sudden proliferation of low amusements downtown probably had a lot to do, first, with the city attorney's investigation in 1859 of the licensing procedures for saloons, billiard halls, and other places of amusement, and, second, with the sabbatarian movement of 1860–61. That amusement areas were more visible and disturbing than ever is evident from the many notices they now received from the newspapers, which seemed almost obsessed with the alleged evils of these places, especially the more "notorious" houses near the depots.[29]

If the drinking and whoring that went on in these places was viewed with disgust, the disorderliness and crime they allegedly engendered was viewed with alarm. This was implicit in the many complaints and the press coverage about "low dens" and other disreputable establishments. Occasionally the point was made quite explicitly. Justice Bagg, for example, in pleading his case for police reform in 1854, singled out houses of prostitution for "the nightly theater of rows inside their crime stained walls" and the "brutality outside of them in the public thoroughfares." Typical was the assertion of the *Free Press* the same year that a recent mugging was probably the work of "some of the ruffians who infest the drinking holes near the river." In a series of articles in 1859 on the "Habitués of the Police Court," the *Free Press* attributed most cases of assault and battery to "rowdies," whom it described as "a class of young men which will always exist in large cities and are fostered mainly by drinking saloons." A Common Council committee reporting on sabbatarian petitions in 1861 recommended that the Sunday law regarding saloons be enforced, since "lawlessness and crime are among us." In 1864, the *Free Press* contended that men who frequented the saloons on "some of the principal streets" were responsible for muggings and molestations downtown.[30]

By the mid–1860s, the Potomac Quarter was the scourge of the city to those prepared to link low-amusement areas to crime and disorderliness. "Murderers, thieves, prostitutes, in short every grade of criminals," wrote the *Free Press* of the Potomac's saloons and brothels, "find in these pit-holes refuge or existence as suits their inclinations or exigencies."[31] After a violent incident in the Potomac in 1863, the *Free Press* reported that "Franklin Street has again added fresh notoriety to its former most notorious reputation as the street which furnishes more food for hungry officers, more 'tangle-leg' whiskey for confirmed vagrants, more victims to the wiles of cunning but frail women, more items for anxious reporters, and finally, more rough and tumble fights, than any other street in the city, if we except its neighbor and twin sister, Atwater street."[32]

In focusing on places of low amusement downtown, law-and-order interests built upon a well-rooted distrust of the transient population, which was generally associated with the same parts of the city. As far back as the 1830s and 1840s, Detroiters commonly attributed crime and disorder to people who were not residents of the city. "At this season of the year," went a common refrain in the *Free Press* (this in the summer of 1845), "we are usually infested with thieves from eastern cities who take up their quarters here until the close of navigation."[33] The crime waves of the 1850s only hardened residents in this belief. The Common Council asserted in 1851 that most criminal offenders "are almost invariably transient persons, not residents of the city of Detroit. . . ." The city clerk concurred. "In most cases," he wrote of those brought before the Mayor's Court for breaches of the peace, "they have been a worthless set of vagabonds of no earthly use to themselves or the community."[34]

By the mid–1850s, the problem of "riotous and drunken vagabonds" assumed even greater proportions. Detroit, as the *Advertiser* admitted, was now a major urban center whose depots and docks brought a never-ending flow of strangers to the city, people who passed in and out of town, many of them rogues of the worst kind. The first group the *Free Press* singled out in 1859 in its series on the "Habitués of the Police Court" were "dock-loafers," whom the paper described as "a class that is indigenous to city life, living by no visible means, sleeping in boxes, barns, stairways, and under sheds on the docks." Later that year the *Free Press* complained that "the docks are lined with greasy looking loafers, who assemble in knots in the shade. . . . Walk the streets at night and you will see many of these men prowling about in a rather suspicious manner; and you will at once make up your mind that they have changed suddenly from day loafers to night thieves." The Civil War supposedly made matters worse. The city now had to contend with draft-dodgers and other transients "set afloat" by the war, as Mayor Kirkland C. Barker complained early in 1865. By now the *Free Press* could announce that Detroit harbored a permanent "floating population," which included "robbers, thieves, and cut-throats in probably a ratio equal to the numbers that inhabit the slums of London and the cellars of Paris." This "class of idle, shiftless vagabonds," the paper went on to say, "can no more live without doing evil and violating the laws that an opium eater can live without his daily dose of poison." Whether it was indicative of the growing numbers of transients in the city, or simply of the growing hostility toward them, vagrants filled the county jail in ever increasing numbers, from only one of every four hundred-fifty commitments in 1847–48 to one of sixty-one in 1853–54 and one of eleven in 1863–64.[35]

Noisy dance halls, cheap brothels, rowdy saloons, drunks and toughs loitering on corners or passing through the downtown from one "low den" to another—all of these attracted the attention of law-and-order interests already upset by mounting crime. The apprehensions of the respectable classes downtown were perhaps never so great as they were in early 1863, when Detroit experienced its most violent riot of the nineteenth century.

Although it was not a draft riot in the same way that New York's famous disturbances of the same year were, the Detroit riot of 1863 traced its origins to the heated issue of military conscription. In the summer of 1862, a mass meeting on the Campus Martius, called to drum up volunteers for the army, had been interrupted by antidraft hecklers. At the close of the meetings they attacked one of the speakers, Eber Ward, who was a Republican and an ardent supporter of the war. While the anxiety about conscription was at that point premature, the demand for manpower and the dwindling of volunteers forced some Michigan counties to begin drafting men by February of 1863. Detroit continued to fill its quotas without resorting to conscription, but there was considerable agitation

in the city, especially as news arrived that the federal government was at work on a national draft law.[36]
The more the city fretted over the war and the draft, the
more visible and offensive to whites the city's blacks became.
Fanning the racist fires was the popular *Free Press*, which joined
other midwestern Democratic newspapers in pursuing a vicious campaign in 1862–63 against Republican handling of the
war. The Emancipation Proclamation, it claimed, made the
draft particularly odious, not only because whites were now being enlisted to liberate blacks, but also because the freedmen
would come north and take away the jobs of those drafted to
free them. The proclamation was simply one of the many mis-
guided "abolition nigger doctrines" responsible in part for a
new "Negro impudence" and "insolence." This was allegedly
exhibited by an increase in open black sexual transgressions,
such as interracial elopements and marriages, which the *Free
Press* reported in provocative detail. By early 1863, the paper
was also complaining more than ever about the various "nigger
dives" on the city's near east side.[37] The racial tensions had
turned to violence as early as the summer of 1862 when a mob
of young whites tried to beat up some blacks near the business
district on the east side. The incident was triggered by a
confrontation the week before between a white soldier and a
black resident of the city.[38]
It was a case of a black man allegedly violating the sacred
sexual code that sparked the massive rioting of 1863. In late
February, a local tavernkeeper named William Faulkner, who
was apparently a mulatto, was charged with molesting two
young girls, one white, the other black. The circumstances
were not altogether clear, and the girls would later confess that
they had lied. Whatever, many Detroiters in early 1863 were
prepared to believe anything if it involved black sexual trans-
gression. Malicious and inflammatory reporting by the *Free
Press* helped to create almost an hysteria over the incident.
"The people had never experienced anything like it," a veteran
newspaperman later recalled. "They regarded it as a bugle call
to battle, rose up *en masse* and screamed for the darky's
blood."[39]

The trial was held at City Hall, on the Campus Martius in the very heart of the city. On the first day, March 5, it attracted a throng of spectators. When Faulkner was escorted back to the jail at the end of the day's proceedings, a crowd estimated at one thousand persons followed and hurled stones at him, knocking the man out at one point. Officials were barely able to get him inside the jail. The next day the city awoke to full details of the new federal conscription law, especially its three-hundred-dollar exemption clause, which was contemptible to the laboring men against whom it discriminated. The rape trial continued, then, in an ever more excitable atmosphere. It attracted a larger crowd this second day, one that overflowed onto the Campus Martius. Even as the trial went on in the courtroom, people outside were beating up blacks who happened to wander by. Word soon filtered out that Faulkner had been judged guilty and sentenced to life imprisonment, the state's maximum penalty. The prosecuting attorney, J. Knox Gavin, who in 1857 had made a feeble case against some of the brothel rioters, was this time merciless in his arguments. But the crowds outside City Hall seemed only more enraged. Officials decided to call in the military Provost Guard from the barracks in order to escort the prisoner back to the jail several blocks away. The guard moved through the crowds only with great difficulty, and just as the soldiers were ushering Faulkner into the jail they leveled their guns at the surging mob and fired a volley, killing one man instantly and wounding several others. The guard then quickly retreated to the barracks.[40]

Many in the crowd were incensed by the shooting. "If we are to be killed up for niggers," one man reportedly yelled, "then we will kill every nigger in this town." Moving off from the jail, located just to the northeast of the business district at Clinton and Beaubien streets, a mob now charged down into the old near east side along Brush, Beaubien, and St. Antoine, where many of the city's blacks lived. Here the rioters assaulted blacks, pelted houses and shops with bricks, and eventually set fire to a number of buildings. As was the case in New York's riot of 1863, the concentration of blacks in Detroit was not so

substantial (nor were blacks so numerous) as to put white mobs
in danger of being trapped in predominantly black neighborhoods, and thus the reckless abandon with which they carried
out their attacks. One black died of his wounds, another score
suffered injuries. Thirty buildings were destroyed by the fires.
Some blacks even fled the city to escape the fury of the mob.[41]

The rioters of 1863 seemed to be of a different stamp from
those who had made life miserable for prostitutes on the outer
east side during the 1850s. First of all, fewer were German.
The violence took place on the near east side, where the
Germans were not so numerous. Even though the only man
killed by the soldiers' volley, a photographer named Charles
Langer, was German, three of the four injured were not. Two
were Irish. Twenty-two men were picked up for rioting by
state troops called into Detroit on the evening of March 6, and
twenty-four more were arrested in the weeks after the violence
(only six were eventually convicted of rioting or assault). Of
these forty-six arrested persons, no more than a half dozen
were clearly German, but at least twenty were Irish. The *Free
Press* at first blamed Germans for the violence, but retracted
the charge the next day. Black victims and eyewitnesses
mentioned the Irish more often than the "Dutch" in their
accounts of the violence. Of the eighteen arrestees who could
be identified from the city directories of 1862 and 1863, at least
four were Irishmen who lived in Corktown, the only ones who
did not reside in the general vicinity of the riot area.[42]

The rioters of 1863 were also, as far as can be determined, a
less "respectable" group than the brothel rioters of the 1850s.
The reports of the antiprostitution disturbances had suggested quite strongly that the mobs were composed of Germans living in the immediate neighborhoods. This was likely to
make them skilled or semiskilled workers, perhaps family men
with their own property. Among the eighteen arrestees in
1863 whose occupations could be ascertained, there were nine
skilled workers, one clerk, one peddler, five laborers, one
sailor, and one soldier. The press singled out two more as
juveniles, and six of the names had more than one entry in the
directories, and so could not be identified. That twenty-one
more names could not be found in the directories at all,

however, is a strong indication that these men were transients, and probably of a lower occupational status. As it was, at least six of those identified were boarders. The newspapers characterized the hard core of the rioters, reportedly less than a hundred men in all, in terms that had become familiar to those who had read articles in the dailies in recent years about crime and disorder. The *Advertiser and Tribune,* for example, described them as "young fellows brought up in the 'street school'—rowdies and vagabonds, ignorant, unreasoning, and crazy with whiskey and prejudice."[43]

What most distinguished these rioters from the neighborhood mobs of the late 1850s, however, was that they showed none of the latter's discipline and restraint. Since the violence of 1863 also took place much closer to truly valuable properties, this was a serious matter and more important than the makeup of the mob. As long as the rioters had stayed well within rundown areas on the near east side there were few efforts to put a stop to the violence on the part of the authorities or bystanders (who included many "respectable" and "prominent" people, according to the newspapers). The fire companies acquiesced in the rioters' demands that they not play water upon buildings set afire. Toward evening, the mobs had drifted quite close to the business district, in fact directly behind City Hall. Here they set fire to a row of buildings inhabited not by blacks, as it turned out, but by "poor white people." Sparks from these fires flew dangerously over a "valuable block of stores" and other important property not far away. A sudden change came over the fire companies, who now worked feverishly to put out the flames. Citizens who had stood idly by before rushed forward to help. The *Free Press* observed that it was a good thing the fire companies had obeyed the earlier demands of the rioters and onlookers, for had they not, their hoses would have been cut and the subsequent fires near the business district would have raged out of control. An eyewitness said that during the violence Fire Marshal William Champ himself admitted to him that "all we can do is to save the property of white citizens." Champ later reported that he and his men had only done what they felt would provide the "greatest good to the greatest number."

The Common Council applauded the firemen "for the energetic and prompt manner in which they so successfully exerted themselves to stay the fearful conflagration which threatened destruction to some of the most valuable and populous portions of this city."[44]

Men of property and standing, even if some of them may have felt little compassion for the city's blacks, were clearly shaken by the disaster that had almost befallen them. They responded much as did the business communities of Philadelphia in 1844 and St. Louis in 1854 when rioting had threatened their properties and investments, and they had found it necessary to think more carefully about matters of city policing.[45] While much of the riot's aftershock consisted of political bickering between aggressive Republican editors and a defensive *Free Press* over the causes of the violence and the ineptitude of Democratic city officials and the police in handling it, there were signs that many prominent citizens wanted no repetition of the frightening scenes of March 6. On the day after the riot, the *Advertiser and Tribune* initiated a call for a public meeting to protest the violence and to take measures against renewed disorder. As the city's principal Republican daily, the *Advertiser and Tribune* was clearly acting from political motives. The *Free Press*, however, made no attempt to brand the meeting a partisan ploy. In fact, along with the *Advertiser and Tribune* it stressed the meeting's bipartisan character and represented its participants as "the very best and most influential citizens." Those mentioned in connection with the meeting were indeed an impressive group. They included Christian H. Buhl, an ex-mayor who was, as will be seen, a leader in the city's police reform movement; Edmund Brush, president of the Board of Water Commissioners and one of the city's most respected citizens, whose homestead encompassed the entire block bounded by Randolph, Croghan, Lafayette, and Brush streets (the last named for his father Elijah Brush) and was located but a short distance from the scene of the rioting; and J. Knox Gavin, Wayne County Prosecuting Attorney and, of course, the prosecutor of Faulkner. Included among the twenty-two men mentioned in connection with the meeting were eight prominent lawyers, seven merchants and manufacturers, two bankers, a major real estate owner, an insurance company executive, and a contractor. Three of the men were members of the Board of Trade.[46] The principal object of the meeting, besides its criticism of the authorities for failing to take "reasonable precaution" during the Faulkner trial, was to call on officials to declare a curfew and to organize a volunteer citizens' patrol, which would serve as a temporary police force until the crisis had passed. Mayor William C. Duncan happened to be in Lansing all this time on official business, and Acting Mayor Francis B. Phelps, a Fourth Ward alderman, was seemingly overwhelmed by the responsibilities he faced during the disorder. Now, perhaps stung by the criticism, he wasted little time in following through on the recommendations of the public meeting. In fact, knowing of the sentiment that was going to be expressed at the meeting, he had anticipated it in moving forward on a special police plan on the morning after the riot. Officials understandably looked to "influential citizens" to volunteer for police duty, but found them reluctant to do so. Most of the men who were listed as police volunteers in the records of the Common Council and who could be identified in the 1863 city directory were manual workers and small shopkeepers. But the Common Council's Committee on Police did report that "a number of the Detroit Board of Trade" served as special policemen on the day after the riot. Under any circumstances, however, the temporary police force (which lasted three weeks) was largely a response by city authorities to the pressure exerted by some of the city's most respected citizens.[47]

Clearly, then, the rioting in March of 1863 made prominent businessmen and professionals more prepared to assume leadership in Detroit's police arrangements in the face of disorder. This was demonstrated later the following year, when rumors abounded that Confederate raiders were poised for an attack on a number of Great Lakes cities, and that disorderly ruffians in the pay of the rebels were already in Detroit ready to disrupt the presidential election. For the latter eventuality city officials organized another special police and called out the local militia. The business community, however, took the initiative in providing Detroit with more substantial protection. The Board of Trade sent the mayor its plan for a larger volunteer force. The mayor in turn passed it on to the Common Council's Committee on Police, which agreed that it "would constitute the most effective and least onerous organization to all property holders and businessmen of the city." The press was also enthusiastic. The *Advertiser and Tribune* thought the new force could not only protect the city in the event of a rebel raid, but could also deal with the city's day-to-day crime and disorder problems. The *Free Press* looked forward to seeing Detroit's "turbulent residents" put in order. When the city disbanded its special police after the election, the *Free Press* declared that the "responsibility for the safety of the city is now in the hands of the Board of Trade, its committees, and the people."[48]

The Board of Trade plan called for a small army of a thousand men—this was, after all, a military exigency—to patrol the riverfront and business district. Once again, businessmen and the fashionable elite showed little interest in offering their personal services. The *Advertiser and Tribune* said that most of the volunteers were "laboring men and mechanics." A list of the men enrolled from the First, Fifth, and Ninth wards (thus, all the west side except Corktown) is available in the city archives. Of those volunteers who could be identified in the 1864 city directory, the bulk were shopkeepers and manual workers. The working-class character of the force meant that most of the men resided in the outer parts of the city. Only four of forty-two names on this list of volunteers, in fact, were from the fashionable First Ward. Consequently, there was considerable friction reported between the men on patrol and the organizers of the force, the Board of Trade. The volunteers had expected to be stationed conveniently near their own neighborhoods, only to find out that they were being sent to the business and fashionable districts. In the meantime, the dreaded rebel raid never materialized. The total strength of the force did not even approach the one thousand men hoped for, and those who were recruited often failed to report for duty. By early 1865 the force was all but disbanded.[49]

The events of 1864, nonetheless, were important in the context of what had been taking place in the city in recent years. After a decade or more of serious crime waves downtown, added to the problem of streetcorner disorderliness that grew during the Civil War years and was compounded by the near-disastrous violence in 1863, Detroit's business and professional communities had developed a sense of responsibility for seeing to their own police needs and to the city's police needs they defined as their own in ways that went beyond the procedures employed on a regular basis by the municipality. Along with the riot the year before, the crisis of 1864 augmented a steady drift among many prominent citizens toward an acceptance of the principle of professional city policing. It was, in fact, the last critical milestone on the road to the complete reorganization of the Detroit police.

THE CREATION OF THE METROPOLITAN POLICE FORCE

The predicament in which the fashionable elite found itself by the 1860s was not unlike that faced by the German neighborhoods a few years earlier. Flanking the business district and even some of the well-to-do residential sections were rapidly growing areas inhabited by a generally lower-class transient population and filled with the disreputable amusements transients patronized. No longer to be dismissed as an ephemeral aberration, these areas were clearly a fixed part of the city's spatial makeup, and they loomed conspicuously in the mental topography of Detroit's leading citizens. As men of property and standing reacted to downtown crime and ruffianism they pointed an accusing finger instinctively at the saloon-vice districts, and the people associated with them. The concern about law and order and the visibility of the disreputable areas reinforced each other. Without the disreputable areas, crime and disorder downtown could not have been so easily explained; without crime and disorder, the disreputable areas could not have become dangerous areas. Thus, like the German community in the 1850s, the elite was fighting off a serious threat to its sense of well-being. Where German mobs resolved the problem with violence, however, the elite responded by finally supporting the organization of a municipal professional police force. The difference was not a measure of group self-restraint or ethical values, but rather one of power. The Germans could achieve only by violence what the elite could achieve through the influence it wielded in the city at large. Both the mob and the police, therefore, emerged as agents of social, or more precisely spatial, control.

The importance of this spatial function in the inspiration for municipal police reform cannot be overstated. If the law-and-order problem involved not only depredations on elite property but also the high visibility of the dangerous elements in certain prominent areas, then the matter of policing had to become more complex. Businessmen who left their shops and offices behind at night when they went home to their comfortable neighborhoods could delegate the protection of their properties downtown to private watchmen. Increasingly that left much of the law-and-order problem uncared for. A force was needed to patrol the whole downtown, where it could work to stem the tide of crime that threatened even some of the nearby fashionable streets, and where it could also control daytime as well as nighttime street life, protecting the respectable classes from the annoyances and criminal actions of people whose growing sub-areas of flophouses, saloons, and brothels might only be reinforcing them in their evil ways. Now the role of the police had been enlarged to a point where private and individualized arrangements appeared woefully inadequate. The police system was to be preventive and supervisory as well as protective. Such a force not only would require discipline and professional commitment, but also would have to draw its authority, and its financial sustenance, from something greater than a small collection of concerned businessmen. So Detroit's men of property and standing turned to the municipality itself, reaching it, as things turned out, through the state legislature.

By the late 1850s, even as police reform lay dormant from the defeats of 1854 and 1856, there were signs that order-conscious citizens were prepared to enhance the municipal prerogative in matters of law and order. Because many Detroiters now believed that the incarceration of arrested and convicted persons often reinforced criminal tendencies, there were sustained efforts to build a city workhouse and to overhaul the delapidated county jail. Both institutions were to be rehabilitative in their designs. When the workhouse proposal first came before the taxpayers in the depression year of 1857, it was voted down, the matter hopelessly mired in a scandal over the proposed site of the institution. In 1859, the workhouse was approved at a citizens' meeting especially well attended by "the substantial men" of the city. The new Detroit House of Correction accepted its first charges in 1861.[50] In the meantime, following a succession of scathing reports by grand juries and the County Supervisors of the Poor, the old jail was torn down and a new one constructed in 1863. An overwhelming affirmative vote in the city had swung the county election of 1860 that authorized the necessary funds.[51]

These efforts helped to prepare some of the groundwork for the movement toward the reorganization of the city's police. Detroit's Republicans were from the start the most outspoken proponents of police reform. The Republican party was strongest in the First, Second, and Fifth wards, which included almost all the business district and fashionable residential sections. The party had a measure of support throughout the city, and in 1860–61 it captured both the mayoralty and the Common Council for the first time. This was a party, as political scholars have shown, that was receptive to the reform spirit, to the rationalization of society in accord with moral values, to the enhancement of the governmental prerogative at all levels in the pursuit of the new order.[52] In his annual messages of 1860 and 1861 the Republican mayor, Christian H. Buhl, who was a downtown hardware merchant, argued that the time had come for Detroit to organize a professional police force. The Common Council, under the yoke of the Republicans, responded with a charter amendment that established the framework for a revamped police system. The Democrats took over the city government in 1862–63 by winning back the outer working-class wards, and the new police provisions were only partially implemented. Detroit now had a Board of Police Commissioners empowered to recommend the appointment of policemen, but none were appointed on a regular basis.[53]

Reformers persisted, however. In February 1863, ex-Mayor Buhl and a group of businessmen petitioned the Common Council to establish a paid police force. The petition went to the council's Committee on Police, which, composed as it was of three Democratic aldermen from the Third, Fourth, and Ninth wards and the Democratic city attorney, was not a committee likely to be particularly enthusiastic about police reform. Yet it emerged deadlocked from its deliberations, suggesting growing sentiment for police changes even among Democrats. Two committee members simply said that the cost of a paid police would be prohibitive; interestingly, they made no effort to deny the need for such a force. The other two members were enthusiastic and specific in their support of the petitioners, taking care to point out that a professional system would actually be cheaper than the current police arrangements. They contended that the city needed a new police to deal with a crime problem of major proportions. "Murder, cold-blooded assassination, burglary, highway robbery, assault upon peaceful unarmed citizens, insult to and assaults upon females upon our most public avenues," they wrote, "to say nothing of the attempted commission of these and other felonies, have been the production of a single night during the passing winter. Crime in our city has become common to the day and the night."[54]

Three weeks later came the race riot of 1863. The *Advertiser and Tribune* hoped the city would learn a lesson from the violence and organize the full-time police system it had long been calling for. Certainly the temporary citizens' police set up in the wake of the riot impressed many people in the city with its effectiveness. There was a brief flurry of activity in the Common Council directed at preparing a new police ordinance, and a month later Alderman Joseph Hoek of the Third Ward, where the riot had taken place, proposed that the controller bring in an estimate on the cost of a night police to be considered at the annual citizens' meeting. Hoek was one of the aldermen who two months earlier had reported adversely on the Buhl police petition. Nothing came of all this, however. The city attorney drew up an ordinance, but the Common Council never acted upon it. In 1863, and again in 1864, the estimates for a regular police force to be considered by the taxpayers apparently never got beyond the Common Council's Ways and Means Committee. The city continued to get by with special temporary forces when needed, such as the policemen appointed in late July and early August 1863, when officials feared draft disturbances in Detroit in the wake of those in New York City.[55] As important as the riot of 1863 was in alerting important downtown property owners to their vulnerability and in awakening the interest of many citizens in the city's police arrangements, it was not followed by any immediate significant changes in Detroit's regular policing.

In the fall of 1864, however, with the city clumsily trying to protect itself in the face of the rebel threat and turning helplessly to the Board of Trade for police initiatives, advocates of police reform finally grew impatient. In early November, the *Advertiser and Tribune* reported that businessmen and big property owners were anxious to see a professonal police force set up. The paper now recommended that the matter be brought to the attention of the state legislature (which just happened to be dominated by Republicans). In January, a petition went to Lansing from a large group of Detroit residents, some of whom may have gone to Lansing in person, calling on the legislature to exercise its authority over the city and establish a full-time professional police force. The petitioners pointed to the city's deteriorating crime condition, in which muggings and burglaries took place even on the most prominent streets. They added that the present police system was inefficient, and they dispensed with the financial question by detailing the money already being expended for special forces and private watchmen. Police advocates were making it clear that they expected any new force to give special attention to the downtown.[56] The names of those who signed the petition were not reported in any of the dailies, nor are they available in the legislature's journals, but the *Free Press* claimed that most were wealthy men who could afford the higher taxes. The driving force behind police reform in the winter of 1864–65, according to Silas Farmer, was John J. Bagley, prominent Republican, ex-alderman from the Third Ward, successful businessman, passionate exponent of a variety of reform causes, and future state governor, who in 1863 could have watched from his house on Macomb Street the mobs following the Provost Guard and the prisoner Faulkner back to the jail. Bagley was one of the founders of the Detroit House of Correction and served on its Board of Inspectors, a group which continually called for police reform in the early 1860s.[57]

Republicans were still clearly the leaders in the movement for a state-controlled police force. It was, in fact, part of the urge in some Republican quarters to give the state a share of responsibility in many of the city's administrative functions, and thereby undermine the power of Detroit's strong Democratic party.[58] Nonetheless, Republican efforts had at least some Democratic support. When police reform talk picked up in November 1864, the *Free Press* called it partisan political opportunism, but quickly backed down the next day. Proponents of the state police plan claimed their ranks were filled with Democrats as well as Republicans. Most importantly, even Democrats who were opposed to the state plan were not necessarily opposed to police reform itself. City officials appeared ready to organize some sort of regular police force. The Common Council sent a police plan of its own to the state legislature in the form of a charter amendment, and Mayor Kirkland C. Barker hoped that the taxpayers would approve funding of a municipal professional police in April 1865. In the meantime, Democratic city officials petitioned the legislature to reject the idea of a state-controlled police. They argued that such a system was inimical to the principles of local governmental autonomy and majority rule, and that it would cost too much, the standard Democratic caveat.[59]

The question of what a new police system would cost and how it would be paid for was, in fact, the key question, the one on which the two sides in the police debate really divided. The *Free Press* would even have been happy to see the state operate a police force in Detroit as long as Lansing footed the bill.[60] The matter of police funding was bound up with the important consideration of who really needed more police protection in Detroit. Under the state's plan, the new police would be supported from the city's general tax fund, and critics charged that this was grossly unfair since it made everybody pay for a service only a few required. Working-class residents in the outer parts of the city had shown little interest in police reform. If they had seemed anxious about a rumored rebel raid, they were not terribly concerned about crime and disorder. A Seventh Ward Democratic alderman complained that the proposed state police force was too large for a city in which the only problem areas were all downtown. His Democratic colleagues agreed. In a set of resolutions promising to institute a legal challenge to the state police, they complained that it was going to be a force distributed primarily in the central parts of the city, thereby abolishing the need for private watchmen, a traditional system "which is just and proper as leaving to the wealthier and more dense portions of the city the care and expense of protecting their own interests in some measure at their exclusive cost." Instead, the new police, performing mostly downtown service, would be supported from the general tax, "paid equally by such portions, *and* those portions that will not receive and do not require such extra protection" [emphasis added]. The Democratic city plan apparently would have left the funding of the police up to the citizens' meeting, along with other taxes, while also expecting downtown interests to supplement the city police with their own privately paid watchmen.[61]

The debate was a lively one, but for opponents of the state plan it proved fruitless. The city's proposal was left to die in legislative committee, while the other sailed through. On the last day of February 1865, without the support of the Democratic representatives from Wayne County, the legislature enacted into law the bill creating the Metropolitan Police Force of the City of Detroit. On May 15, uniformed, professional policemen began patrolling the streets of Detroit on a regular basis for the first time in the city's history.[62]

The story of Detroit's struggle to establish a professional police system allows us to answer the questions with which we began. Crime and disorder were indeed important in Detroit's police reform movement, but they were important not because they occurred at what were in fact unprecedented rates. Rather, the significance of crime and disorder was in *where* they occurred. Detroit's most prominent and influential citizens, living and working in the downtown area, were threatened and often victimized by criminals and toughs as much as, if not more so than, any other group in the city, certainly any group with a modicum of political clout. The working classes showed little interest in police reform. For them, especially the immigrants, the police only represented a potential threat to their drinking customs. Police reformers in Detroit, who were led by downtown businessmen and professionals, therefore spoke with conviction about the threat of crime and disorder in the city. Such talk was not a smoke screen for more tyrannical designs. A few police reformers no doubt were moved by authoritarian urges, and under any circumstances the new police force was meant to control one segment of society for the benefit of another, but the propertied elite, working mostly through the Republican party to give Detroit a professional police, was only protecting itself from what it perceived to be real danger.

When reformers and order-minded citizens looked for the sources of the crime and ruffianism all around them, they were conditioned in their response by the changing spatial organization of the downtown. Like urban elites elsewhere Detroit's had formed an impression of a dangerous class. It was a class feared most for what it was already responsible for in the way of crime and disorder, and its identity was clear to concerned Detroiters. The term *dangerous class* was actually seldom used. More common were *loafers, saloon loungers, vagrants,* and similar terms, which were far more descriptive of the elements respectable citizens truly considered dangerous. Loafers, loungers, and drifters had in common their association with certain parts of the city, namely the low-amusement districts in and around the downtown. Detroiters feared as much a "dangerous area" as a "dangerous class." The spatial exclusivity that the elite had achieved in its residential style had also been achieved by the dissolute transients the elite distrusted, and in the process these dangerous people seemed that much less controllable through traditional methods of order-keeping.

Since, then, the crisis in law and order was to a degree a spatial one, the new professional police idea had a powerful logic. There were advantages to the well-defined spatial arrangements downtown once the commitment was made to restore order. A preventive police could work that much more effectively if the dangerous elements confined themselves to circumscribed areas; and key properties and important citizens could be that much better protected if they, too, were confined to certain areas. In short, the spatial patterns that had been a liability could be turned into an asset in the struggle against crime and disorder when the professional police was brought into the picture.

Police reform in Detroit, therefore, cannot be reduced to any simple class, ethnic, or political-ideological interpretation. Law-and-order interests were not preoccupied with the working class in general. Even the casual laborer posed no distinct threat if he was a married man with a family living in a single-family dwelling. Ethnicity rarely figured in the arguments of police reformers. No one was prepared to think of crime and disorder as an Irish or a German problem, or even an immigrant problem. Everybody had placed the responsibility for the prostitution violence on the doorstep of the German community, but this was violence few considered as part of the law-and-order crisis. And the attempt to link the Germans to the racial disorder of 1863, which was indeed part of the law-and-order crisis, was feeble and short-lived. Finally, if Republicans were chiefly responsible for engineering state intervention into Detroit's police matters, Democrats were nonetheless by then at least on record in support of police reorganization, and the principal issue was really one of means, not ends.

The extent to which spatial development had a hand in the concern for law and order in Detroit suggests something about why the timing and the logic of police reform differed among various cities—even as they all made the move to professionalism during the middle part of the nineteenth century. If we want to find out why it was that St. Louis organized a modern police system a full ten years after New York, and why its respectable classes worried more about transients and idlers than the Irish immigrants New Yorkers apparently feared most, then we might learn much by comparing the spatial evolution of each city in addition to the social or economic characteristics.[63] An appreciation of the spatial variable, in fact, can be a start in the formulation of a comprehensive interpretation of urban police reform in the nineteenth century. This is not to say that we can ignore other factors. Clearly, police reform was not unrelated to the wider concern for social control that had roots in traditional American ideology, in ethnic heterogeneity, in early industrialization, or in the reform spirit of the age, and which found expression in everything from educational innovation to the rise of the Republican party. One cannot ignore, however, that changing spatial patterns in the growing cities of the nineteenth century complicated, even undermined, traditional methods of social control. There was an inextricable connection between the city's geography and the development of an institution that would have as its most novel and salient feature the daily supervision of urban space by the cop on the beat.

FOUR

The Professional Police and the City

Detroit's new police department went to work in a city that
during the 1860s and 1870s expanded considerably in the
wake of population growth, the rise of new heavy industries,
and the introduction of the horse-drawn trolley. The physical
sprawl of the city did not alter the basic patterns in land use
that had emerged by the early 1860s. The spatial differentiation in the old central part of the city that had been so critical in
the drive to establish a professional city police force remained
mostly as it was and served as the basis for the department's
modus operandi in its early years. It was, in fact, the continuing
spatial dimension attributed to the city's dangerous class that
facilitated police handling of what respectable citizens viewed
as the most serious threat to law and order in Detroit by the
1870s—the "tramp problem." In the process, the new patrolmen enjoyed a public legitimacy that made almost uneventful
the transition to police professionalism.

SPATIAL PATTERNS IN THE EARLY STREETCAR ERA

In the decade after 1864, Detroit doubled its population to
become a metropolis of over one hundred thousand people. It
continued to function as a regional entrepot and a transfer
point on major east-west trade routes, but Detroit was now
clearly more than just a commercial center. By 1868, the city's
twenty leading manufacturers had an annual output valued at

six million dollars. Like many cities in the Great Lakes area, Detroit specialized in iron and steel products, in this case steam engines, stoves, and railroad cars and wheels. The Peninsular Car Works in Detroit was actually the largest factory of its kind in the country. It employed fifteen hundred men in 1882, when it turned out six thousand railroad cars. Herein lay the basis for Detroit's later rise as the home of the automobile industry.[1]

The population growth and economic development of Detroit in the 1860s and 1870s were accompanied, as they were in other large American cities in these years, by an early form of urban sprawl. Few people lived more than a mile and a half from Detroit's City Hall in 1860, but by the 1880s major residential tracts stretched out three miles and beyond (Maps IV–1, IV–2).[2] A principal agent of Detroit's spatial growth, though by no means the only one, was the horse-drawn streetcar which first appeared on the city's streets in 1863. Early trolley lines radiated from the central business district like the spokes of a wheel. Streetcars proved to be a popular innovation in the city's transportation and by the mid–1870s were carrying almost three million passengers annually.[3] Real estate promoters rushed to offer lots in hitherto undesirable or inaccessible outer areas, often advertising the proximity of their tracts to existing or contemplated trolley lines. "All the attractions of a home in the heart of the city, without its disadvantages," one ad read. While not all the real estate promotions were successful, there were reports as early as four months after the introduction of the streetcars that land sales and land values in outer areas were increasing rapidly. The extension of the city's residential space came almost entirely in the form of single-family houses. The ratio of persons per dwelling in the city changed little between 1860 and 1880 as Detroit continued to absorb additional residents without crowding them into multi-family "tenements."[4]

The expansion of the city ruffled the patterns of residence, but did not alter them significantly. The older, compact, fashionable areas began to stretch outward in the 1860s along Fort and Lafayette streets to the west, Woodward and Cass to the north, and Jefferson Avenue to the east. By the late 1870s, the

MAP IV–1: Detroit, 1863. *(Burton Historical Collection.)*

elite concentration along the upper sections of Woodward and
Cass had acquired the sobriquet "Piety Hill" (though it was
hardly a hill) and was challenging Fort Street West as the most
prestigious of the city's residential neighborhoods. Nonetheless, most of Detroit's well-to-do residents continued to live in
or near the established fashionable areas, and even the newer
wealthy neighborhoods were extensions of the old, remaining
physically and emotionally attached to the heart of the city.[5]
Working-class families owned or rented the majority of houses
in the residential periphery. Some lots in the streetcar sub-
divisions sold for as little as fifty dollars down in 1866, and
workingmen were encouraged by real estate ads to take
advantage of the chance to gain an attractive urban homestead. Unpretentious frame cottages could be built on the lots
for a modest cost. With just one hundred and fifty dollars, for

MAP IV-2: Detroit, 1886. *(Burton Historical Collection.)*

example, one could buy all the requisite lumber. It was not uncommon for purchasers of single lots to construct the cottages with their own hands, thereby saving on additional labor costs. Blacks appeared to have the fewest residential options. The corridor of black settlement between Woodward Avenue and Hastings Street on the east side now stretched to the upper reaches of the city and the so-called Kentucky district around Kentucky Street, but most blacks still lived on the lower east side, and only a few well-to-do blacks were able to break out of the narrow corridor itself.[6]

The outward movement of the population created new secondary business districts in the form of commercial strips along major streetcar lines, particularly those passing through the immigrant working-class neighborhoods in the north-eastern and northwestern parts of the city.[7] The central business district, meanwhile, continued to grow and expand. Newer and bigger warehouses lined the riverfront. Banking, insurance, and legal services took over Griswold Street, to the west of Woodward. Major retail stores crowded Jefferson and Woodward, the latter all the way to the Grand Circus, close to a mile from the river. The large department store made its first appearance on Woodward, exemplifying the growing sophistication of the business district. The passing away of a number of stubborn old landholders—"men of means who had an attachment to their landed patrimony that outweighted their desire to see Detroit become a metropolitan city," wrote one city booster—led to the development of several centrally located but formerly unimproved lots.[8] More than ever, the central downtown stood as the focal point of the city, the source of elite pride. In 1869, its role as cultural center was enhanced by the construction on the Campus Martius of an opera house dressed in stylish French mansard garb. Then in 1871, a new City Hall was completed just across the square. In the French style, yet beautifully eclectic, the building dwarfed the old neoclassical City Hall constructed in 1835 and symbolized the added responsibilities and complexity of municipal government, as well as the vitality of the heart of the city.[9]

Scattered about the central business district and surrounding areas were many of the city's principal factories. There was one particularly large concentration near the Michigan Central depot. Yet the linear spatial needs of manufacturing, the importance of immediate access to major forms of transportation, and, in some cases, the desire to escape high property taxes, all combined to make the city's factories more dispersed than commercial activity. Light industry, such as chemicals, boots and shoes, and tobacco products, as well as a portion of Detroit's heavy industry, stoves for instance, located throughout the lower east side, especially along the riverfront, out to the city limits and beyond. In fact, three of every four persons employed in manufacturing in 1874 worked in the riverfront wards on the east side. By the 1880s, however, Detroit's burgeoning railroad car and wheel industry and some of its other heavy manufacturing had located strategically near big railroad junctions at the extreme western and northeastern ends of the city. The gravitation of many factories to the urban periphery was probably as important as the streetcar in the development of outlying working-class residential neighborhoods. Many people lived in these new neighborhoods not because they could now use the streetcar to ride to work downtown, but rather so that they could be within walking distance of the factories on the city's fringe.[10]

Despite the emergence of these peripheral manufacturing complexes, as well as the new secondary business districts, the great bulk of the city's jobs, of all kinds, existed in the area extending from the vicinity of the Campus Martius down to the riverfront between the depots, and then eastward to the city limits. And most people still came into and went out of Detroit by way of the downtown docks and depots. Thus the central parts of the city, especially the lower east side, remained attractive living space for the many employed and unemployed transient workers in the city, as well as unmarried men generally, whether from Detroit or elsewhere. Accordingly, boarding houses, cheap hotels, and saloon flophouses, which continued to proliferate in the 1860s and 1870s, were located mostly in and around the heart of the city, with the largest concentrations on the lower east side.[11] An important development in the housing of transient males, one that perhaps indicated both their growing numbers and their declining fortunes, came in the late 1870s with the appearance of the simple "lodging house." Unlike the boarding house, it offered rooms on a day-to-day basis, no meals included. The price was usually cheap—five or ten cents per night. Without a dining area or parlor, the lodging house had none of the pretenses to domesticity and respectability that the boarding house often had. Lodging or rooming houses became popular in many cities beginning in the 1870s.[12]

The amusements associated with the bachelor and transient subculture in Detroit, not surprisingly, remained clustered predominantly in the downtown as well, as Map IV–3 shows.[13] To be sure, the growth of working-class neighborhoods and the emergence of the streetcar commercial strips carried more and more saloons out beyond the heart of the city, particularly on the densely populated German east side, where taverns and beer halls seemed to be on every corner. Much of the retail liquor trade, however, was still around the business district, the depots, the boarding houses, and on the near east side generally. Detroit's vice areas, in the meantime, had actually become more concentrated. The near east side from the river to Gratiot Street continued to stagnate. Even the fashionable residential area just to the east of the business district along Jefferson began to break up. The whole area was dotted with decaying older structures. The expansion of the central business district was mostly to the north, and few legitimate businesses sought space to the east. Flophouses, saloons, but, above all, brothels rushed into the vacuum as the rest of the city left the old near east side behind. The Potomac Quarter, and now also the "Heights" between Jefferson and Gratiot, dominated the landscape of vice in Detroit into the early 1880s, while throughout these years, the brothel district on the lower west side remained only a minor center, hemmed in by the depot, the river, the business district, and the mansions of Fort, Congress, and Lafayette streets.[14]

Because social and business space in the center of Detroit was arranged in the late 1860s and the 1870s much as it had been before, when it had served as a catalyst for police reform, the geography of the law-and-order problem in these years had a familiar look. More than ever, in fact, the respectable

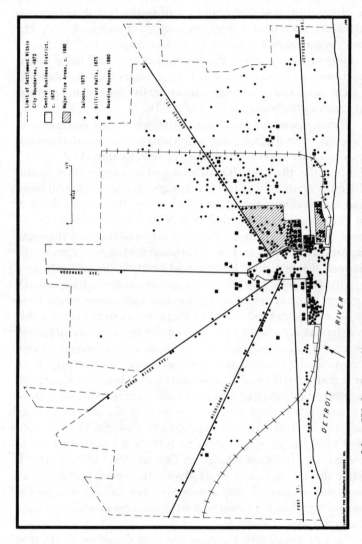

MAP IV–3: Boarding Houses, Saloons, Billiard Halls, and Vice
Areas, 1875.

classes associated criminals and ruffians with the transient, low-amusement areas, particularly on the east side. It was in the Potomac Quarter where one allegedly could find "the worst species of outlaws," where roosted the city's "thugs, confidence men, burglars, and murderers," or where "the vilest thieves, pimps and cutthroats" resorted.[15] In a colorful piece entitled "The Dark Side of Metropolitan Life," the *Detroit Evening News* in 1875 pinpointed the city's most disreputable and dangerous areas. In addition to the Potomac, there was "Niggertown" around Fort and Beaubien streets on the east side; also the vicinity of the Michigan Central depot on the west side, especially along Front Street, where the most sordid "rookeries" were "mostly boardin' houses, and the unfortunate who enters one of them for lodging is 'boarded' until he is drunk, and then is robbed, carried to any convenient lumber yard, and dropped." A year later, the *Free Press* described the Fort-Beaubien neighborhood as "one of the most disreputable in the city, and a criminal who once secrets himself in any of the low doggeries there need feel no uneasiness, as he is sure to be well shielded by the vagabonds who spend most of their time there."[16] This public consensus about where one could find Detroit's most dangerous characters was to shape the organization and administration of the city's new police department, as well as the behavior of its men on patrol. If nothing else, it would make the department's job seem that much easier to officials and citizenry alike.

THE NEW POLICE AND THE SPATIAL ORDER

Born of the wedlock between important downtown interests and the Republican party, Detroit's Metropolitan Police Department was, from its inception, in the care of the city's business and professional community. The state appointed the Board of Police Commissioners, but all four members of the board had to be Detroit residents. The men who served as commissioners during the early years of the department were, in the words of one mayor, "gentlemen of the highest integrity, thorough business men." When a Detroit attorney wrote a

letter of recommendation in 1877 for a nominee to the board
he took pains to point out that the man was "widely known in
manufacturing, banking, & social circles." Eight of the nine
men who sat on the board between 1865 and 1885 were downtown businessmen; the other was a fashionable lawyer. Until
1873, the board was dominated by John J. Bagley, the prominent manufacturer who had been the leader of the police
reform drive, and who personally prepared the new department's rules and regulations in 1865.[17]

The commissioners reviewed every application to the force
and decided which men would serve in the department.
Surviving manuscript police records provide information on
all the men (265) who were appointed between 1865 and 1871
(Table IV–1). Policemen came from a slightly higher occupational background than might be expected given the occupational breakdown of all employed males in Detroit of their
general age group. The force consisted predominantly of men
who had been manual workers, the bulk of them skilled.
Scattered evidence on other mid-nineteenth-century police
forces shows similar occupational backgrounds among the
personnel. A two-year Michigan residency requirement for
Detroit policemen, meant to discriminate against transients,
seemed in the process to discriminate against common laborers and other marginal workers. At the same time, police
salaries did not attract those with the highest manual skills.
Patrolmen earned more than laborers and about the same as
carpenters, but they made less than machinists. The force had
a disproportionate number of native-born recruits, a product
in part of the citizenship requirement and the English pro-
ficiency test, which contributed to the striking underrepresen-
tation of Germans on the force. That the Irish were over-represented is perhaps further evidence of the traditional proclivity
they are supposed to have had for police work. During the
mid-nineteenth century the Irish were also well represented
on the New York and St. Louis police forces, for example,
while the Germans generally were not.[18]

The residential patterns of Detroit's police appointees reflected their other characteristics. Since the force was composed mostly of working-class men (three-fourths of whom

The Professional Police and the City 97

TABLE IV-1: PERCENTAGE DISTRIBUTION OF POLICE AP-
POINTEES BY OCCUPATION AND PLACE OF
BIRTH, 1865–71

	Policemen	All Employed Males in Detroit Aged 16–59, 1870[a]	All Employed Persons, Detroit, 1870[c]
Professional	1	2	
Proprietor	17[b]	13	
White collar	10	14	
Skilled	41	38	
Semiskilled	16	8	
Unskilled	14	24	
United States	54		39
Germany	6		26
Ireland	25		14
British America	4		10
Great Britain	8		10
Other	2		1

[a]Occupation categories in aggregate census data were occasionally unclear and every effort was made to be judicious in fitting them into those used here.

[b]Includes a number of "farmers"—men who may have come to Detroit from the countryside in order to become policemen.

[c]Here, and in the tables to follow, an error obviously made by compilers of 1870 census data involving domestic servants employed in Detroit was corrected by making estimates based on 1880 census data.

SOURCES: Force Roster and Record Book "A" (1865–71), PD/CA; U.S. Census Office, Statistics of the Population of the United States (Washington: Government Printing Office, 1872), p. 785.

were married, many with children), policemen tended to come from the outer residential areas. Because the force had so few Germans, relatively few appointees lived on the outer east side, even though it was more heavily populated than the west side. In the immediate preprofessional police era, before the dramatic outward growth of the city in the late 1860s, policemen had been more likely to live closer to the center of the city, even in and around some of the principal vice districts on the east side. In all, over half of the deputies and specials appointed in 1861–63 resided on the east side, while only about a third of the professionals appointed in 1865–71 did (Map IV–4).[19]

How much the socioeconomic, ethnic, and residential characteristics of the new police force were by design of the commissioners and how much they were the result of other factors is difficult to determine. The commissioners knew from the application forms the occupations, ethnicity, marital status, and home addresses of all the men whom they appointed to the force. There is no evidence that the commissioners also conducted personal interviews. Whatever the case, however, the new police force comprised what the commissioners must have considered a respectable and trustworthy group of men—men who were generally not associated with lower-class transient elements, nor with the areas those elements favored. If law and order was to be reestablished in Detroit, the new professionals would be just the men for the job.

The police department quickly demonstrated that it viewed its principal function as service to elite interests downtown. As expected, the new professional system was almost another version of the old "Merchants' Police," with the added responsibility of watching over the dangerous areas. One of the first things department officials instructed patrolmen to do was copy down the names of prominent businessmen on the main commercial streets, along with their home addresses, so that the department could easily reach these citizens when any problem arose. If patrolmen, furthermore, were to be pulled from their beats for service elsewhere, the beats were to be those with the fewest stores and businesses.[20] The only police station between 1865 and 1873 was located in the heart of the central business district, and only five blocks from the Potomac Quarter. The department built two new stations in 1873 on the east and west sides of the city, and several substations followed in the outer areas over the next half-dozen years. Still, most patrolmen remained downtown. In 1876, half of the force worked out of the original central station, and another 30 percent out of the station on the disreputable east side. That same year the commissioners defined the area of most importance to the police as the business district within a half-mile

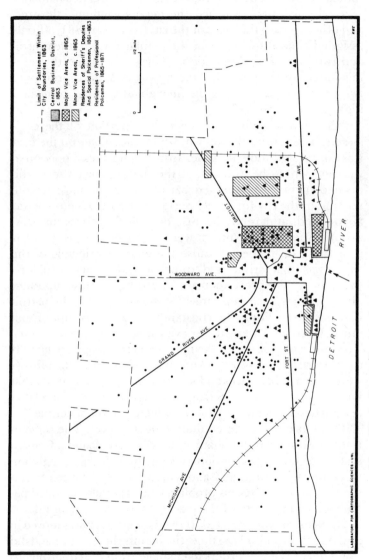

MAP IV-4: Preprofessional and Professional Police Residences, 1861–71.

radius of the foot of Woodward. Almost all the department's "special policemen" watched the depots, landings, theatres, and other spots in the heart of the city. As late as 1881, officials assigned almost two-thirds of the regular force to the central and two lower-east-side stations. Three years later, the commissioners stated flatly that the department gave priority to two factors in distributing the men about the city: crime and high property values.[21]

Policemen actually patrolled only a portion of the city's streets. These were downtown, where the officer on the beat was considered indispensable. In the outer areas, policemen were merely to be available at the stations for citizens who needed them.[22] (A mounted patrol served the most remote sections of the city for a brief period in the 1870s before it was abandoned, apparently because officials felt it was unnecessary.)[23] The men downtown were to patrol, not just wait for something to happen, because the guiding principle of the force was that crime and disorder should and could be prevented. "The prevention of crime being the most important object in view," the department's *Manual* began, "the patrolman's exertions must be constantly used to accomplish that end." Patrolmen were to do even more than make arrests. They were to get to know their beats and the people in them. If there were any persons "of known bad character," the officers were to learn their faces and watch them "in such manner that it will be evident to said persons that they are watched, and that certain detection must follow the attempt to commit crime."[24]

This was easier ordered than done, however. The conventional wisdom was that many criminals were floaters. Could a system of crime prevention relying upon facial recognition work in such a fluid and anonymous society? Police officials seemed to recognize this problem when they also directed patrolmen to take note of the places where criminal and disorderly elements congregated. If the dangerous classes moved in and out of the city all the time, the haunts they frequented did not. One of the first orders to emanate from the superintendent's office, in fact, was that patrolmen report all the places on their beats likely to be the resort of criminals, gamblers, prostitutes, or disorderly persons. Similar orders came down in later years. Lists of these suspicious places were to be kept at the superintendent's office and posted where all patrolmen could see them.[25]

One of these lists has survived. Dated November 1866, it included "twice-reported" houses of ill fame, as well as gambling dens, disorderly and after-hours saloons, "suspicious houses," and dwellings where stolen goods were likely to be secreted.[26] The locations of these places are revealing (Map IV–5). They were concentrated mostly in the lower east side, with subcenters near the Michigan Central depot and along one of the streetcar commercial strips on the west side. These areas corresponded generally with the transient amusement areas most associated by law-and-order interests with criminal and disorderly elements. Although similar lists are not available for later years, the police department did publish in its annual reports of 1878 and 1879 the breakdown by precinct of brothels, disorderly houses, and other places of questionable character. Almost all of them turned up in the central or east-side precincts. While this does not pinpoint them very accurately, it still suggests a locational pattern similar to that of the 1866 list.[27] In 1879, the *Free Press* reported that policemen were also beginning to keep a close watch on the new "cheap lodging houses" as likely hangouts for thieves and cut-throats. The lodging houses of concern to the police were located in the old disreputable streets just to the east of the central business district above Jefferson Avenue.[28]

That the police located most criminal resorts and suspicious places in the traditionally disreputable sections of the inner city may simply have been because so many patrolmen walked beats in and around these areas. Nonetheless, from any standpoint the spatial dimension of Detroit's policing was clear. The department served the elite interests downtown that were struggling with well-defined dangerous areas. Policemen, recruited mostly from outer working-class districts, were stationed in the central parts of the city to patrol the business district and nearby disreputable quarters. Responding to the needs of those who employed them, policemen found the sources of crime and disorder in the same neighborhoods that had worried police reformers and continued to concern order-

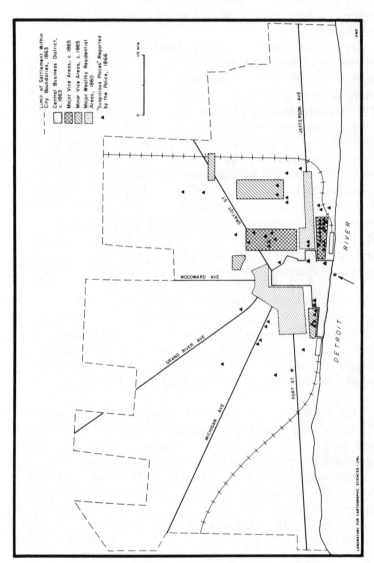

MAP IV–5: Suspicious Places Reported by the Police, 1866.

minded citizens. Such a police force working downtown was a great relief to fashionable citizens. Dangerous areas were not so dangerous if patrolmen could serve as a buffer between them and important and valuable properties.

Since the police in a way depended upon disreputable haunts in the campaign against crime and disorder, we would expect that department officials could tolerate their existence as long as the public was convinced such places were under control and supervision. This may well explain why the police department in Detroit (and departments elsewhere, for that matter) was willing to live with segregated red-light districts by the 1870s. Houses of prostitution had always been the bane of order-minded citizens, who viewed them not only as dens of immorality but also as centers and breeders of crime. Police officials and their men recognized this. The bulk of the places included in the 1866 list were brothels. In its early years the department actually pursued a vigorous policy against vice, directing its attention mostly toward lower-class bordellos. The "descent" became one of the most well-publicized of police activities. The superintendent himself led some raids to dramatize their importance. One sortie into the vice districts in 1866, for example, took patrolmen to twenty houses of ill fame, where they made over fifty arrests.[29] Correction officials were so enthused by all this that they lobbied successfully for a state law in 1869 that mandated a three-year term at the Detroit House of Correction for convicted prostitutes over the age of fifteen. The object was to incarcerate the prostitute long enough to reform her. When the law was passed, officials at the House of Correction claimed that over one hundred prostitutes fled the city.[30]

By the middle of the 1870s, however, the police were assuming a much less aggressive stance toward prostitution. Compared to the 1857–72 era, the newspapers now reported few raids. Police arrests for prostitution declined to a mere trickle. From highs of 239 and 143 in 1869 and 1872, they fell to 17 and 11 in 1875 and 1876. According to the *Evening News* in 1875, the current police policy was only to raid brothels "where overt acts of disorder are committed."[31] By then the department had shown that it was watching brothels closely and that the public need not worry. In the meantime, the seemingly un-controlled expansion of vice downtown that had so profoundly disturbed the respectable classes in the early 1860s had given way to a measure of stability. The prostitution district on the west side remained a minor one, while the Potomac Quarter filled out a bit, but in an area that at this point was not of much interest to legitimate business; nor was it near elite residences on the east side, most of which were farther out along Jefferson. So everyone was happy. The police had criminal hangouts to turn to, the respectable classes had a sense of order and security, and the prostitutes had a place to ply their trade.

PUBLIC ORDER ARRESTS AND THE TRAMP PROBLEM

Although order-minded citizens were put at ease by the extent to which low amusements and cheap boarding and lodging houses remained within the general areas they had already appropriated in the early 1860s and were watched closely by the new professional policemen, by no means did they feel that the people who drifted through these areas were to be overlooked. The respectable classes in Detroit had long pointed to "loafers" and "vagabonds" as one key to the city's crime and disorder. The "floating population" dilemma took on new meaning as a consequence of the national depression of 1873–78, which forced even more American males than usual to become peripatetic in the search for jobs. Unemployment everywhere rose precipitously. It was estimated, for example, that one of every four workingmen in New York City was without a job in the winter of 1874–75. The movement of unemployed men from place to place was most common in the line of states from Massachusetts to Illinois, the heart of urban-industrial America, and the area served best by transportation systems. The transient armies of the 1870s seemed to urban elites, including Detroit's, to be like so many locusts descending upon their communities. The image of the desperate, deceitful, and thieving jobless migrant assumed added clarity and made the pejorative term *tramp* part of the national lexicon.[32]

By late 1873 in Detroit, many workers had already been out of work for as long as six weeks, and the *Free Press* reported that applications for poor relief in the city had risen sharply.[33] Sympathetic though Detroiters were with the plight of the poor and the unemployed within the city, they now seemed to feel that many of the city's indigent lived as they did because they wished to, not because of economic circumstances beyond their control. Some felt that there were too many ways for professional beggars and the chronically unemployed to sustain themselves in the city without working. City officials and the newspapers called for a House of Industry to which such people could be sent and put to work. Also, Detroit's various private charities formed a single association in the late 1870s to coordinate their efforts and prevent abuse of their good will by those they sought to help.[34] The distrust of the city's poor grew in direct proportion to the fear that the city was overrun with tramps, a term Detroit embraced as readily as any community. The consensus was that tramps had no intention of working, in or out of a House of Industry. The *Free Press* called them "idle, filthy, worthless fellows," and a prominent Detroit philanthropist added that they were "bold, shameless, and boisterous" good-for-nothings who made a mockery of the charitable impulse.[35]

Citizens now found it that much easier to view transients, or the "idleness and unemployment" they personified, as the source of the city's crime and disorder. After the late 1860s, it became common for the newspapers to blame tramps and other elements of the floating population for petty thefts and burglaries, as well as for more serious offenses like mugging and drunken disorderliness. After one rash of street robberies in December 1869, the *Free Press* pointed out that because navigation had ended for the winter and sailors and others were bottled up in the city, there were "hundreds of ugly faces loafing about that bear the word villain in characters plain to be read, and belonging to men who travel from one city to another for villainous purposes." The House of Correction supposedly compounded matters by continually discharging into the city its criminal vagrants, many of whom were origin-

ally from other parts of the state, but who now, according to
Mayor Hugh Moffat in 1873, were "let loose upon this city to
swell the proportion of that class of her inhabitants." If nothing else, citizens found tramps offensive by their mere presence in the city, especially if they went about the streets beg-
ging.[36]

The Metropolitan Police had to handle the problem of vagrants and tramps to the satisfaction of the respectable classes.
The department indirectly served this end by opening the
doors of its station houses at night to destitute people. By
the early 1870s, this practice was straining police facilities, and
the central station had to be remodeled to accommodate the
"homeless, houseless army" who made use of police beds. Officials felt that this served as a check on crime, however, and
some suggested that Detroit follow the example of other cities
in providing soup and bread for lodgers as well. In the meantime, overnight lodgers inundated the police stations. From
less than five hundred in 1865–66, the number soared to over
twenty-six hundred in 1869–70, over seven thousand in the depression year, 1874–75, and eleven thousand in 1879–80.
Ninety-five percent of the lodgers were males.[37]

The drifter who showed up at the police station for a night's
lodging was one thing. Quite another was the vagrant who preferred the streets and the saloons, and who was perhaps already contemplating a criminal act. Professional policing offered the hope that these people could be removed from the
streets. The old constabulary had not patrolled the city with
any regularity. Deputies had spent most of their time chasing
down suspects for crimes already committed. They picked up
dangerous drunks and vagrants only if of a mind to, if the fee
was worth it, or if a complaint had been lodged. The new professional patrolmen, on the other hand, pursued a more aggressive policy of routine order-maintenance, in which discretionary "public order" arrests for the offenses of drunkenness,
disorderly conduct, disturbing the peace, and vagrancy played
a central part. Police reformers had this in mind when they
conceived of a professional force. The new patrolmen were to
rescue the principal streets of the downtown from the riffraff.

That the professionals would make more arrests for public order offenses seemed assured by the idea of crime prevention. Since a patrolman's efficiency was ideally measured by the absence of crime on his beat, a point made explicitly in the department's *Manual*, then it made sense to him to arrest criminals before they could act; and were not drunks and drifters the source of most of Detroit's crime and disorder? If there was any doubt about the legality of the aggressive policy of order-maintenance, it was removed at the start, in late 1865, when a local justice ruled that the new professionals could jail a person for drunkenness without first filing a complaint. Also, in the 1870s changes in city and state law made loitering and vagrancy more explicitly violations against public order. Policemen could now move against loafers and drifters as never before.[38]

Patrolmen were in a good position to deal forcefully with the problem of vagrants and transients through public order arrests because they were stationed disproportionately in those parts of the city where tramps tended to congregate and where many transients, seasonal workers, and the unemployed had always concentrated—around the depots, the railyards, the docks, and throughout the cheap boardinghouse and low-amusement districts. The *Detroit Post* in 1875 described one place near the Michigan Central depot as "but a fair sample of the doggeries which infest the vicinity of the riverfront. It combines the worst qualities of a rough boarding house and low saloon, and the proprietor depends chiefly for his income upon the hard earnings of sailors, men who, as a class, are proverbially improvident and prone to squander their slender wages in drink and dissipation." The *Free Press* reported in late 1878 that "homeless, reckless, and penniless men" filled up "every low groggery and sixth-rate boarding saloon" in the downtown. During the daytime, idle men often wandered around the nearby business district. A favorite spot was Grand Circus Park, just to the north of the major retail stores on Woodward, and bordering on some of the most fashionable residential streets in the city. "The lazy loafers lounging around on the grass and benches," the police superintendent complained in 1870, "are becoming so impudent that respectable persons cannot enter the park without being insulted." Although a few tramp settlements appeared on the outskirts of the city in the 1870s, most transients and men out of work still flocked to the central parts of the city.[39]

The new professional policemen in Detroit, like their counterparts in other cities, made many more initiative arrests—arrests for public order offenses—than the preprofessional constabulary ever had.[40] In a two-year period from 1862 to 1864 the constables, deputies, and special policemen in Detroit had sent a total of 803 persons to the Police Court for such offenses.[41] By comparison, in the first ten months alone, the professionals made over twelve hundred arrests for public order offenses. From 1867 to 1870, these averaged over eighteen hundred per year, and by the depression years of 1873 and 1874 the annual figure was up to thirty-five hundred (Table IV–2). A precipitous decline in drunk and disorderly arrests around 1876 may have been related to the enforcement of a tough Sunday saloon law passed by the state in 1875. Mayor Alexander Lewis claimed as much in 1877 when he vetoed a Common Council resolution permitting the saloons to open once again.[42]

Throughout these years, the campaign against vagrants and tramps, as carried out by the police in the form of public order arrests, received additional impetus from the reaction of the respectable classes to the growing problem of working-class radicalism. Solid citizens in Detroit viewed strikers and other labor agitators as but a step removed from vagrants and tramps—lazy and deceitful men who hoped to undermine the system of free labor in which workingmen toiled for whomever they wished and for whatever wage they were willing to accept. Workers' organizations and management, therefore, were essentially incompatible. "No man can serve two masters," the *Free Press* argued in the face of a strike by its own printers in 1867. The worst venom was always reserved for strikers, especially during the difficult summer of 1877 with its threat of violence in conjunction with railroad work stoppages. Although there were no disturbances in Detroit, as there were in so many cities, the press was ready to condemn workers for any

TABLE IV–2: PUBLIC ORDER ARRESTS, 1865–80

Year	Drunkenness	Disorderly and Disturbing the Peace	Vagrancy	Total
1865–66[a]	670	504	65	1,239
1866–67	N/A	N/A	N/A	N/A
1867–68	1,174	681	118	1,973
1868–69	1,155	461	141	1,757
1869–70	1,050	482	163	1,695
1870–71	1,041	693	160	1,894
1871–72	1,436	864	151	2,451
1872–73	1,710	870	109	2,689
1873–74	2,221	1,189	236	3,546
1874–75	1,840	1,332	328	3,500
1875–76	1,263	1,002	375	2,640
1876–77	994	793	443	2,230
1877–78	1,078	892	849	2,819
1878–79	1,301	865	449	2,615
1879–80	1,332	821	225	2,378

[a] Ten months only.
SOURCE: *Repts. Police Comm.* (1866–80).

trouble whatsoever. Disorderly workers, according to the *Post,* were to a man "tramps, bummers, and vagrants." The *Free Press* exhorted the authorities to be prepared for violence. "The whole moral and physical force of the community," it wrote, "must be brought to bear promptly and effectively in checking and preventing any spread of the evil, and in meting out deserved punishment to the violators of the law and of the public peace."[43]

The police responded with disciplined action against troublesome workers. In 1868, the department answered the call of the captain of a steamer who wanted policemen to protect dockworkers from striking longshoremen as they unloaded his cargo. In 1874, street and sewer workers marched around the city trying to work up a general strike to protest the shortage of municipal jobs. At several locations they roughed up men who did not wish to leave their work and join the dissidents. The police moved in quickly. The ringleaders were arrested, the others frustrated in their efforts to organize several demonstrations, and special squads of police were sent to guard street workers on the job.[44] When Michigan Central Railroad workers struck at the downtown depot in the summer of 1877, the Board of Trade formed a "Protective Association" to move against any mob violence. The police welcomed this, and also encouraged concerned citizens to enroll with the department as emergency volunteers. Three hundred special policemen were also called out, and patrolmen watched over a local trades' union meeting while a large force stood by at a nearby station house.[45] Finally, the superintendent ordered patrolmen to clear their beats of all "tramps, vagrants, and known thieves," and to break up any suspicious streetcorner gatherings and discussions "that will tend to excite disturbances or riot." The newspapers reported that policemen in carrying out this order focused largely on the transient areas near the riverfront and on the east side. In only two days they arrested forty persons for vagrancy, thirty-four of these in the central precinct and the remaining six in the east-side precinct. Vagrancy arrests for the year 1877–78, as Table IV–2 shows, were nearly double those of the preceding and following years, as the police responded both to the anxieties of the respectable classes and the ill fortunes of casual labor.[46]

What sort of people did policemen arrest in their vigorous efforts to maintain routine public order in downtown streets? We can refine the analysis of police arrests by using systematic samples of all arrested persons, drawn from the manuscript police blotters kept by the department from its inception in 1865. The samples cover two-year periods; the first in 1869–71, and the other in 1879–81, each period coinciding with years for which federal census data are available for comparative purposes.[47] Table IV–3 reveals that people arrested for public order offenses were more likely than those arrested for other offenses to be from the lowest occupational groups, that is, semiskilled and unskilled manual workers. More significantly, they were almost twice as likely to be true transients— people with no local address to report to the police clerk, who usually just put "None" in the blotter for the residence of these arrestees. It seems likely that during the depression years of

TABLE IV-3: PERCENTAGE DISTRIBUTION OF PUBLIC ORDER
AND NON-PUBLIC ORDER ARRESTEES BY OCCU-
PATION AND RESIDENCE, 1869-71, 1879-81

| | 1869-71 | | |
	Public Order Arrestees (N=444)	All Other Arrestees (N=424)	All Employed Persons, Detroit, 1870
Professional	2	1	3
Proprietor	7	13[b]	11
White collar	3	3	11
Skilled	26	25	30
Semiskilled	22	17	26
Unskilled	24	17	19
Other[a]	16	24	—
No local address	N/A	N/A	—

| | 1879-81 | | |
	Public Order Arrestees (N=572)	All Other Arrestees (N=346)	All Employed Persons, Detroit, 1880
Professional	1	1	3
Proprietor	5	17[b]	13
White collar	3	4	15
Skilled	28	21	33
Semiskilled	22	18	23
Unskilled	29	19	13
Other[a]	13	20	—
No local address	44	24	—

[a]Includes housekeepers, students, juveniles, no occupation, and prostitutes
(1879-81 only).

[b]Includes large number of saloonkeepers arrested for various liquor law
violations.

SOURCES: Sample data, 1869-71, 1879-81; U.S. Census Office, *Statistics of
the Population of the United States* (Washington: Government Printing Office,
1872), p. 785; U.S. Census Office, *Statistics of the Population of the United States*
(Washington: Government Printing Office, 1883), p. 876.

the 1870s, when public order arrests rose dramatically in an atmosphere of growing concern about tramps, the percentage of those arrested with no local address was even higher. Three of every four arrests for public order offenses in 1879–81 were reported in the central precinct, which helps explain why so many arrestees were drifters.[48]

Thus, the Metropolitan Police made initiative arrests of people who generally fit the popular image of the dangerous elements: lower-class transients. As Arthur Stinchcombe has pointed out, there is always a class bias built into an order-maintenance arrest policy, since the lower classes generally do not have access to private places in their daily socializing the way the middle and upper classes do. Consequently, they are more vulnerable to the scrutiny of police officers. In the same way, homeless men are more likely to be arrested for vagrancy, and if they are drunk, more likely to be arrested for drunkenness than the local resident, who might simply be sent or escorted home, especially if he is a "respectable" citizen.[49]

The ethnic distribution of public order arrestees, as Table IV–4 shows, was not unlike that of policemen themselves, in particular the over-representation of Irish and the under-representation of Germans, a pattern that was to a lesser extent true of all other arrestees. One reason for this was that far fewer Germans seemed to be drifters. Only 5 percent of *all* arrestees with no local address were Germans, while close to 25 percent were Irish. Moreover, Detroit's Germans were residentially segregated and had many neighborhood amusement centers. True, the police watched the German taverns and beer halls closely but this was for Sunday or after-hours violations, not as part of the general campaign against the dangerous class that focused on downtown areas. The Irish, on the other hand, were not as concentrated, nor did they have a neighborhood institution like the beer hall. In fact, there were comparatively few saloons in Corktown. Local Irish males may have been more likely, therefore, to turn up in downtown saloons and other public places, where they would be in a position to be arrested by patrolmen.

Were those whom the police arrested for public order offenses in the interest of crime control and the public peace, fin-

TABLE IV-4: PERCENTAGE DISTRIBUTION OF PUBLIC ORDER
AND NON-PUBLIC ORDER ARRESTEES BY PLACE
OF BIRTH, 1869-71, 1879-81

	1869-71		
	Public Order Arrestees	All Other Arrestees	All Employed Persons, Detroit, 1870
United States	36	45	39
Ireland	30	17	14
Germany	9	15	26
British America	10	14	10
Great Britain	11	6	10
Other	3	3	1

	1879-81		
	Public Order Arrestees	All Other Arrestees	All Employed Persons, Detroit, 1880
United States	45	53	46
Ireland	26	12	8
Germany	6	15	22
British America	11	12	13
Great Britain	9	5	7
Other	3	3	5

SOURCES: Sample data, 1869-71, 1879-81; U.S. Census Office, *Statistics of the Population of the United States* (Washington: Government Printing Office, 1872), p. 785; U.S. Census Office, *Statistics of the Population of the United States* (Washington: Government Printing Office, 1883), p. 876.

ally, the kind of people who were in fact committing the burglaries, larcenies, and assaults that so concerned the respectable classes? Table IV-5 shows that offenders for these serious crimes were less likely to be semiskilled and unskilled workers than public order arrestees, and only half as likely to be out-of-towners. Furthermore, as Table IV-6 indicates, the native-born and the Germans were under-arrested and the Irish over-arrested for public order offenses, given what seemed to be their propensities for criminal activity. The Irish, though

TABLE IV–5: PERCENTAGE DISTRIBUTION OF PUBLIC ORDER
ARRESTEES AND OFFENDERS FOR CRIMES OF
THEFT AND PERSONAL VIOLENCE BY OCCUPA-
TION AND RESIDENCE, 1869–71, 1879–81

	1869–71		
	Public Order Arrestees	Offenders— Theft/Violence[a] (N=123)	All Employed Persons, Detroit, 1870
Professional	2	1	2
Proprietor	7	7	11
White collar	3	3	11
Skilled	26	32	30
Semiskilled	22	15	26
Unskilled	24	20	19
Other	16	24	—
No local address	N/A	N/A	—

	1879–81		
	Public Order Arrestees	Offenders— Theft/Violence[a] (N=133)	All Employed Persons, Detroit, 1880
Professional	1	0	3
Proprietor	5	9	13
White collar	3	3	15
Skilled	28	26	33
Semiskilled	22	17	23
Unskilled	29	24	13
Other	13	21	—
No local address	44	23	—

[a]Arrestees who were actually convicted of these crimes, or the final disposition of whose cases was not recorded in the General Ledger (these latter were few, however).

SOURCES: Sample data, 1869–71, 1879–81; U.S. Census Office, *Statistics of the Population of the United States* (Washington: Government Printing Office, 1872), p. 785; U.S. Census Office, *Statistics of the Population of the United States* (Washington: Government Printing Office, 1883), p. 876.

TABLE IV–6: PERCENTAGE DISTRIBUTION OF PUBLIC ORDER ARRESTEES AND OFFENDERS FOR CRIMES OF THEFT AND PERSONAL VIOLENCE BY PLACE OF BIRTH, 1869–71, 1879–81

	1869–71		
	Public Order Arrestees	Offenders— Theft/Violence	All Employed Persons, Detroit, 1870
United States	36	50	39
Ireland	30	15	14
Germany	9	12	26
British America	10	14	10
Great Britain	11	7	10
Other	3	2	1

	1879–81		
	Public Order Arrestees	Offenders— Theft/Violence	All Employed Persons, Detroit, 1880
United States	45	55	46
Ireland	26	11	8
Germany	6	17	22
British America	11	12	13
Great Britain	9	5	7
Other	3	1	5

SOURCES: Sample data, 1869–71, 1879–81; U.S. Census Office, *Statistics of the Population of the United States* (Washington: Government Printing Office, 1872), p. 785; U.S. Census Office, *Statistics of the Population of the United States* (Washington: Government Printing Office, 1883), p. 876.

conspicuous and disorderly in their drinking habits, were not disproportionately represented among more serious offenders; the Germans, though rarely drunk, disorderly, or vagrant, were more commonly guilty of serious offenses; and the native-born, though often drunk or vagrant, were even more often burglars or assaulters, disproportionately so, in fact. If the police department ever studied its arrest data closely, then, it would have reached the conclusion that patrolmen seeking to curtail serious crime through public order arrests were hauling in many of the wrong people. As a start, they could have paid closer attention to native-born Detroit residents and less attention to Irish tramps.

THE LEGITIMATION OF THE PROFESSIONAL POLICE

When the Metropolitan Police took the streets in May 1865, lingering opposition to the new force came primarily from Democratic politicians who resented the Republican state legislature's intrusion into Detroit's administrative and financial affairs. Opponents tested the constitutionality of the police measure, but were disappointed in October 1865, when the State Supreme Court upheld the law. Some bitterness remained. Detroit's police law was the focus of debate at Michigan's constitutional convention in 1867. During the proceedings, the prominent Detroit lawyer, G. V. N. Lothrop, a Democrat, ridiculed the city's state-imposed police force as an unnecessary collection of "elegantly formed and well-dressed gentlemen." Detroiters continued to complain about the state's interference in their police matters. Typical was the Common Council's assertion in 1876 that "it is a fallacy to suppose that the State is more interested in the good government and management of the police force than the people of Detroit, whose rights of person and property the force is designed to protect. . . ." Detroit would have to wait until 1891 to regain full control over its police.[50]

Vocal opposition to the police in its early years, however, was limited almost entirely to the question of the state's usurpation of municipal power. If there were some who resented the idea of a Board of Police Commissioners appointed from Lansing, there seemed to be no one who felt that the appointees were incompetent. In fact, all agreed that the commissioners were to a man excellent choices, and that the force was on the whole well managed. Both political parties, it might be recalled, had been ready for some sort of police reform in 1865, and the new professionals were expected to serve the downtown interests that everyone admitted needed special protection. If controversial in principle, the Metropolitan Police force was uncontroversial in operation. The Board of Commissioners could assert truthfully in its very first annual report that early opposition to the force had melted away in the face of the department's obvious "effectiveness and value."[51]

The respectable classes supported the police department in its principal endeavor, which was the control of the downtown, particularly the close supervision of the disreputable transient and low-amusement areas. They seemed to feel much as do certain law-and-order interests in today's cities about the requirements of policing in black ghettoes and skid rows. In dealing with Detroit's dangerous class, policemen were to be resolute and forceful. The newspapers rallied behind the officer on the beat in his daily struggle with criminal and disorderly elements. Toughs on the lower east side tried to intimidate the new policemen when they first appeared on the streets, and the dailies encouraged the department to respond aggressively. When one officer was manhandled by a group of ruffians, the *Free Press* remarked that "his duty in the premises was plain, and had he put a bullet through the first rowdy who laid hands on him, he would have rid the community of a blackguard and saved himself from a beating."[52]

Patrolmen were, in fact, not issued revolvers. Yet they were not forbidden to carry one of their own pistols. Officials warned, however, that they should use them "at their peril," since the department would assume no responsibility if an "accident" occurred. In his study of the New York police, Wilbur R. Miller found that the middle and upper classes in that city expected policemen to be tough in dealing with dangerous elements, even if it meant resorting to firearms. While this was also the case in Detroit, policemen were not really expected to brandish firearms on a routine basis in their control of the streets. In the 1870s, there were enough minor incidents of patrolmen using their revolvers without sufficient justification that the press of both parties complained specifically about it. The *Free Press* even suggested that the department forbid officers to carry guns, certainly concealed ones, which was a common practice among patrolmen. That a gun was not considered indispensable to efficient policing in Detroit may have been due in part to the fact that the dangerous class there was not well armed. Only one of every one hundred arrested persons carried a gun, and only one of eight even had a knife.[53]

The policeman's club, on the other hand, was standard equipment, and he was expected to use it if necessary in making arrests. Department officials carefully defined the circumstances in which use of the club was acceptable, however. Patrolmen, for their part, were hesitant to employ force when dealing with people who might make complaints. Publicized cases of police brutality, such as the alleged beating of a ward collector and his two sons in a German neighborhood in 1874, were uncommon enough to suggest they were indicative neither of routine brutality nor popular preoccupation with police abuses. Out of a total of 849 policemen brought before the commissioners for misbehavior from 1865 to 1885, only fifty-two were accused of physically abusing a citizen, an arrestee, or a jailed prisoner. The police surgeon could still claim in 1868 that he had yet to dress the wounds of a person injured by a patrolman's club.[54] How liberal policemen were in their use of the club when dealing with the inarticulate and powerless transient class is difficult to determine. Drunks and tramps were usually not in a position to make complaints about police brutality, and if they did, their cases were not likely to be brought to light in the press. However violent the police were in their routine supervision of the dangerous areas and the streets downtown, it was not a matter of public controversy. The respectable classes, to be sure, did not feel that policemen were any too violent in dealing with criminal, disorderly, and vagrant persons.

Patrolmen themselves offered no serious resistance to departmental policy concerning the control of the downtown. Morale was generally high, insubordination mostly trivial. Instances of patrolmen neglecting their duties led to the great majority of disciplinary cases, but these were not a symptom of any massive evasion of responsibility or antagonism to departmental directives among the patrolmen. They were simply cases of men who could not resist the temptation to duck into a friendly saloon or to catch a few winks on a slow night. There were no publicized cases of patrolmen speaking out against officials on matters related to essential police strategy. The minutes of the commissioners' meetings and the orders coming down to the men through the command structure give little indication that patrolmen were not generally doing what they were supposed to do. The commissioners even claimed in 1878 that a recent case of a patrolman flatly refusing to issue a complaint to a saloonkeeper was the first such case of insubordination in the department's history.[55] If a salient feature of the new professional police was an increase in order-maintenance discretionary arrests, then, it was due not only to the designs of reformers and police officials, but also to the obedience and perhaps inclination of patrolmen themselves.

The harmony between the goals of the command structure and the efforts of the men on patrol was an impressive achievement from today's perspective. Patrolmen tend to develop codes for street and arrest behavior through on-the-job experience rather than in response to departmental directives. Standards learned at the precinct level are usually more elastic and discretionary than those set by the command structure, which are often more for public consumption. The upper echelon of a department cannot always articulate and establish guidelines applicable to the variety of situations the patrolman finds on the street. In short, "professional" behavior, whatever it may be, has to come from the bottom up, not from the top down.[56] In the early years of Detroit's police department, the official code and that of the patrolman on the beat seemed fairly close. It reflected the consensus that prevailed about the sources of crime and disorder and about what the police had to do to serve those most threatened by crime and disorder.

It is perhaps not so surprising, therefore, that Irish policemen and those from the lowest occupational backgrounds were just as diligent, in fact even more diligent, than native-born policemen and those from higher occupational backgrounds in making public order arrests, in which the Irish and the lower classes were over-represented. In fact, Irish policemen were more aggressive even when the drunks or the vagrants they were arresting were their own countrymen (Table IV-7). Miller found that New York's Irish policemen were also more than willing to arrest other Irishmen. It may have been that the Irish policeman simply adopted the attitudes and

TABLE IV–7: SELECTED ARREST PATTERNS OF POLICEMEN BY
            OCCUPATIONAL BACKGROUND AND PLACE OF
            BIRTH, 1869–71

Arresting Officer	Total Arrests (N=868)	Public Order Arrests	Public Order Arrests with Irish Arrestee
Semiskilled or unskilled	222	137 (62%)	—
Other	546	289 (53%)	—
No information[a]	100	18 (18%)	—
Irish	260	177 (68%)	53 (20%)
Native-born	388	180 (46%)	59 (15%)

[a]Some of these were policemen whose occupation was not recorded in the
roster book and could not be found in the city directories. But most were
detectives, who were not included in the roster book and who made almost no
public order arrests anyway.

SOURCES: Sample data, 1869–71; Force Roster and Record Book, "A"
(1865–71), PD/CA.

values of the dominant classes that employed him, while he
also found release for the tensions built up by his self-hatred
and insecurity as a member of a subordinate and much-
maligned group. Miller adds that the Irish cop had a special
propensity for aggressive behavior whenever he dealt with
other Irishmen on the street.[57] It should also be kept in mind,
however, that, at least in Detroit in these years, patrolmen were
making most arrests in areas in which they did not live and with
which they could not even identify. If they adopted a bias
shared by the elite, it was a bias against the disreputable areas
and the people in them. Most patrolmen were neither guard-
ians of friendly neighborhoods nor disinterested agents of an
impartial order. They worked in certain parts of the city almost
as an army of occupation, and because of this, making discretionary arrests was much easier for all patrolmen, whatever
their personal makeup.

FIVE
The Return to Order

By the standards of 1860, Detroit in 1880 was a model of law and order. No longer did mobs, corner toughs, and lurking garrotters preoccupy the citizen as they had before. If much of this had to do with the feeling of security and the image of order provided by the professional police force, it was also because serious crime and disorder had declined markedly. In the 1850s and 1860s, the city's spatial development had contributed to the breakdown in law and order and the anxiety of respectable Detroiters. By the 1870s, it had alleviated neighborhood tensions, created few new environments especially conducive to criminal activity, and helped make it possible for the police to serve as an effective deterrent to crime.

MOB VIOLENCE IN THE STREETCAR CITY

From 1849 to 1863, there had been a dozen major riots in Detroit and probably a dozen other minor ones. Most of these disorders occurred in or near the immigrant residential neighborhoods that were then forming in a variegated and compact urban environment. People attacked what they saw as serious threats to the neighborhood communities they were trying to establish. Houses of prostitution, often catering to blacks, simply had no place on the German outer east side in the late 1850s. After 1863, however, mob violence in Detroit all but disappeared. The few minor disturbances that did occur sprang from different sources than before. Only one had anything to do with the neighborhood issues so prominent in the 1850s—

that, an isolated incident in 1875 when a crowd tore up a block of railroad track. Tent-preaching temperancites and Germans clashed in 1867, a mob threatened to lynch the murderer of a local businessman in 1869, and the supporters of two competing streetcar companies fought over the laying of track on a downtown street in 1876.[1]

Only the rise of labor discontent, manifested in the disturbances by the street and sewer workers in 1874 and the tensions during the railroad strike of 1877, seemed capable of generating violence the way the competition for neighborhood space had earlier. Labor violence, however, was not social violence. The day-to-day living that brought blacks and prostitutes into contact with those who loathed them filled the air with a constant tension. The result was not just chronic disorder of a serious nature, but also countless minor incidents. Disgruntled workers, on the other hand, were not as spontaneously combustible; the potential for labor disorder did not exist every day on countless streetcorners, and striking workers did not descend on the fashionable residences of the capitalist class with bricks and torches in hand.

The disorders and near-disorders of the years after 1865, therefore, posed fewer problems for policemen. Where the deputies had trouble anticipating the riots of the 1850s and early 1860s, and when facing the mobs were ambivalent about them, the professionals moved swiftly against disorderly crowds, even when violence was but a threat, as in 1877. If the new patrolmen responded to riots in a more disciplined manner than their predecessors, it was not simply because the Metropolitan Police Department was better organized than the old constabulary. It was also because the professionals understood better whom they represented, while rioters were no longer engaging in such publicly acceptable and unpredictable exercises as the pummeling of blacks or the stoning of whores. Vigorous action by the professional police in the face of disorder may well have kept some riots from becoming more serious than they were.

The absence by the 1870s of the kinds of neighborhood disorder that characterized the earlier period has a simple explanation. The outward growth of working-class residential areas, increasing racial segregation, and the solidification of the downtown vice districts all served to separate most blacks and prostitutes from those who were hostile to them. Between 1865 and 1880, there was not a single disturbance involving race or prostitution even significant enough to be reported in the newspapers. None of the city's new or maturing older neighborhoods had to compete for space with noisy and disorderly brothels as had the German neighborhoods of the 1850s. The racial boundaries that had yet to be resolved in the rapidly growing and changing city of the 1850s, when interracial houses of prostitution served as the apparent vanguard for black residential settlement, were far more fixed and agreed-upon by the 1880s. When Polish immigrants began arriving in the city during the 1870s, they settled in the northeastern sections of the city. The poorest of them lived near the black Kentucky district, but the majority resided in areas without blacks, or their dance halls, along the upper ends of Russell and Riopelle streets.[2] If the Poles had encountered the blacks and their amusements, or the threat of black residential encroachment, in the same way the Germans had thirty years earlier, violence might easily have resulted, especially since the Poles probably competed with blacks for jobs, far more so than the Germans ever had.

There may have been another way in which the city's spatial development helped to reduce disorder. The Board of Trade believed that the pacifying effect of widespread homeownership in the new streetcar neighborhoods frustrated rabble rousers in the city during the labor troubles of 1877.[3] One is reminded again of the *Free Press*'s contention that homeowners were more law-abiding citizens. It may well have been that working-class urbanites who moved into what were relatively spacious new neighborhoods and lived in single-family cottages (even if they did not own them), at a time when the detached house was the ideal of the respectable classes, felt more a part of the dominant order and therefore less inclined to use violence as a tool for solving problems. But the argument can be overstated. Probably no working-class group in the 1850s had enjoyed the benefits of neighborhood and homeownership more than the Germans, and yet they were the most disorderly group in the city. In fact, strong attachment to the neighborhood among property owners actually contributed to the violence of the 1850s. Residential expansion in the late 1860s and the 1870s was important in the reduction of disorder not for the refinement it supposedly wrought but, again, for the way it kept certain people apart from each other.

PATTERNS OF CRIME IN THE STREETCAR CITY

"The madness of the times has reached and permeates all classes of crime and outlawry," reported the *Free Press* in late 1865. "Base men are lurking in streets and alleys, prowling about our dwellings, lying in wait with greedy eye and murderous hand, with bludgeon, bullet and dagger, to seize their victim, and barter their souls for unlawful gain." Overwrought as this was, it was consistent with general press opinion in Detroit that crime was as serious a problem in the latter half of the 1860s as it ever had been. One of the most frequent explanations offered for this was that the end of the Civil War had thrown back into society thousands of men psychologically damaged by the violence of the battlefield, and otherwise demoralized and corrupted by their military experience.[4] Although there was probably some truth to this, it was a shortsighted argument, for in proper perspective the crime wave of the postwar years emerges as only an extension of the larger crime wave that began in the late 1840s. It did not last long in any case. By the 1870s, newspaper reports of serious crime appeared much less frequently. Hardly to be found anymore were the articles about Detroit's prowling cut-throats and thieving "Break o' Day Johnnies" that had filled the columns of the daily sheets in the 1860s. A substantial drop in the crime rate is suggested further by police statistics on arraignments and arrests (Table V–1). The rates for theft and, even more so, crimes of violence declined steadily after 1865 and leveled off by the early 1870s at rates below those of the 1850s and 1860s. The decline is even more impressive considering that the availability of policemen and police service afforded by the new professional system undoubtedly made crime victims more disposed than ever to make complaints leading to arrests.

TABLE V-1: POLICE COURT ARRAIGNMENTS AND POLICE ARRESTS FOR CRIMES OF THEFT AND PERSONAL VIOLENCE AND FOR PUBLIC ORDER OFFENSES, 1854–85

(PER THOUSAND CAPITA)

Year	Theft	Personal Violence	Public Order
1854–55	6.8	11.1	7.9
1855–56	4.9	8.9	4.5
1856–57	4.9	8.2	4.3
1857–58	5.7	13.4	10.2
1862–63	6.5	12.9	9.6
1863–64	6.5	13.0	5.9
Preprofessional			
Professional			
1865–66[a]	9.2	12.5	21.0
1866–67	N/A	N/A	N/A
1867–68	7.9	12.0	29.4
1868–69	7.6	8.6	24.4
1869–70	6.3	7.8	22.0
1870–71	6.4	7.3	22.8
1871–72	5.0	5.7	28.2
1872–73	3.3	3.6	28.9
1873–74	4.0	3.9	37.2
1874–75	5.8	3.9	34.3
1875–76	5.5	4.0	25.1
1876–77	5.8	4.1	20.8
1877-78	6.0	5.0	25.6
1878–79	5.4	4.4	22.3
1879–80	5.1	4.0	20.7
1880–81	4.5	4.2	23.5
1881–82	4.6	3.6	23.3
1882–83	4.2	3.1	26.6
1883–84	4.3	3.3	34.1
1884–85	4.8	3.1	34.6

[a]Ten months only.

SOURCES: *Free Press,* July 6, 1855, July 11, 1856, July 4, 1857, July 2, 1858, January 6, April 15, July 4, October 8, 1863, January 7, April 4, July 6, October 16, 1864; *Rept. Police Comm.* (1866–85).

Order-minded interests in Detroit had always believed the downtown disreputable areas that first became conspicuous in the 1850s were the source of the city's crime problem. That criminals frequented these transient-amusement areas seemed to respectable citizens self-evident. For one thing, criminals were people who were by nature rootless and dissolute. For another, disreputable areas had a lot of crime, and did it not make sense that where crime was, criminals were not far away? This being the case, the crime problem in the central business district was traceable to the disreputable neighborhoods around it. Burglars and muggers supposedly sallied forth from the transient amusement areas, invaded prominent and respectable streets nearby, did their work, and then slipped back before anyone knew what had happened.

When the new professional police force was organized it was expected to do something about this problem. The department responded by saturating the downtown with patrolmen, who would not only deter criminals by their presence, but would also pursue a vigorous policy of order-maintenance that would catch criminals in its wide net of streetcorner arrests. Once on the streets, the patrolmen may well have come to feel, as policemen do today, that such arrests also prevented crime by removing potential victims from the streets. Hauling drunks and tramps off to the station, that is, was really for their own protection, since the helpless inebriate or "bummer" was an inviting target for the mugger. Criminals in early twentieth-century Boston were supposed to have gravitated to cheap rooming-house districts because they found the transients who stayed there the easiest to victimize.[5]

Whatever the logic was for the Detroit police department's vigorous policy of public order arrests, there seems every reason to believe that these arrests, along with the provisions made for overnight lodgers, helped to cut down on the total amount of crime occurring in Detroit. Even if, as we have seen, patrolmen were sweeping the streets of many people who were not necessarily those most likely to commit serious crimes, there were undoubtedly others hauled in who were. How much these public order arrests had to do with the steady drop in crime, though, is another matter. Serious crime rates in the first eight years of professional policing fell spectacularly, yet public order arrests fluctuated during the same period. In fact, a comparison of the rates for public order arrests and serious crime arrests for the entire 1865–85 period (Table V–1) shows no precise inverse relationship, nothing to indicate indisputably that whenever the police arrested more drunks and vagrants the fewer arrests they had to make that same year for burglary or assault. Patrolmen probably made as many public order arrests in the Potomac Quarter in the early years of the department as anywhere, yet serious crime continued to be a feature of the area until the late 1870s, when it finally tapered off amid the general decline of the quarter.[6] The aggressive order-maintenance arrest policy of the police department probably had more to do with an abatement of disorderliness and ruffianism than burglary and mugging.

Easier to determine is the effect the police had on the spatial patterns of crime. There is no doubt that patrolmen were a deterrent to crime in the central business district, where the preventive concept proved workable. The department made its most concerted efforts there. Every block was covered by a beat. Patrolmen criss-crossed the commercial streets and warehouse districts, peering through windows, checking doors, and walking down back alleys. The effect was immediate. Only a few months after patrolmen first appeared on the streets, the press was already reporting a noticeable decrease in burglaries and muggings on the principal downtown streets.[7] Yet if the police presence in the central business district kept at least some criminals from acting, others were merely inconvenienced. The decline in crime in the business district was accompanied by a reported increase in crime in nearby areas, particularly the fashionable residential neighborhoods. Despite the interest the police department had in protecting these neighborhoods, they were not as easy to supervise as the more compact central business district, to which, in addition, a greater proportion of patrolmen were assigned. By the middle of the 1870s, the newer elite residential sections were asking for more police protection, and the department responded by building substations nearby. Well-to-do residents in these outer areas seemed as much concerned about routine disorderliness as serious crime. For example, petitions to the police department from fashionable property owners along Jefferson Avenue where it sliced through the manufacturing districts on the outer east side wanted more patrolmen to keep an eye on the many "mechanics and laborers" who worked in the vicinity. Nonetheless, all reports suggest a growing crime problem in prominent residential districts.[8]

Map V–1 shows the locations of crimes of theft and personal violence reported and pinpointed in every other issue of the *Free Press* during the year 1878.[9] Crime continued to occur frequently in the central business district. Burglaries still plagued the retail stores and the warehouses, and muggings still awaited the unwary at night. However, considering the expansion of the business district and particularly the great increase in retail establishments, including the new department stores, it seems clear that the incidence of crime there had diminished since the 1860s and that the saturation of the area by the police was at least partly responsible for it. In the meantime, burglars were now working regularly in the elite residential neighborhoods, including the newly formed ones adjacent to the disreputable upper near east side. Detroit's well-to-do had merely traded one problem for another. The introduction of a professional police force helped to keep a few burglars and muggers away from their businesses and offices downtown, but it was unable to prevent, in fact it probably encouraged, the spread of crime into some of their residential neighborhoods. On the whole, one's property was most insecure in the business district, the fashionable neighborhoods, and the disreputable streets of the near east side; one's person most unsafe in the low-amusement quarters near the depots and the boarding and lodging houses, and in the Kentucky district on the upper east side.

A rather simple logic can be used to explain these crime patterns. Burglars struck where the most valuable property was, muggers where people were likely to be unwary or careless. It was a logic police officials themselves used in stationing their men and combatting crime. The intriguing thing, then, is that crime was still most prevalent—even if it may have been diminished—in those parts of the city in which the police presence

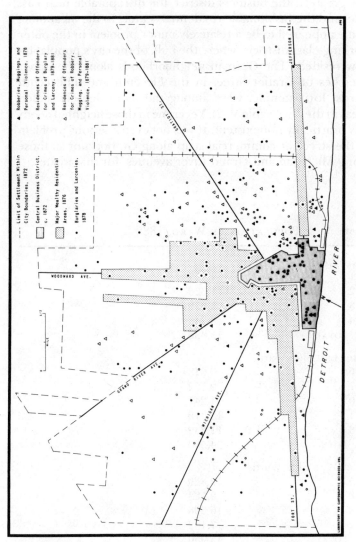

MAP V–1: Patterns of Crime and Criminal Residence, 1878–81.

was greatest: the business district, the disreputable near east side, and the fashionable residential center. In the meantime, crime appeared to be a relatively minor problem in the outer working-class districts, where the bulk of the city's population now resided. The German neighborhoods along the upper stretches of Gratiot Street in the Eleventh and Thirteenth wards, for example, were among the more densely settled areas in the city (Table V–2). Yet crime in those neighborhoods was practically nonexistent. It was not even a serious problem in the streetcar commercial strip along Gratiot, nor in those along Michigan and Grand River avenues, for that matter.

TABLE V–2: POPULATION BY WARD, 1880

Lower Central Wards	
1	4,777
2	1,329
3	3,979
4	5,745
TOTAL	15,830
Outer East Side Wards	
6	9,618
7	9,152
10	11,241
11	13,310
13	11,239
TOTAL	54,560
Outer West Side Wards	
5	12,829
8	9,723
9	16,296
12	7,102
TOTAL	45,950
CITY TOTAL	116,340

SOURCE: U.S. Census Office, *Statistics of the Population of the United States* (Washington: Government Printing Office, 1883), p. 221.

Jane Jacobs, in *The Death and Life of Great American Cities,* speaks of a crime deterrent built into the structure and character of certain neighborhoods—animated neighborhoods in which at any given time local residents are casually watching and surveying the goings-on from their windows, their porches, or their stoops. These "eyes on the street" serve as a form of policing that helps make for a safer environment.[10] It seems possible—and this is highly speculative—that the working-class sections of late nineteenth-century Detroit were the sort of neighborhoods Jacobs is talking about. For example, unlike most stores downtown, those along the streetcar lines in the working-class areas were open at night to accommodate the people in the surrounding neighborhoods.[11] The streets were alive with activity well after dark, posing far more problems perhaps for burglars and muggers than did the empty streets of the central business district back in the 1850s and 1860s, or some of the spacious fashionable areas of the 1870s. Even after the stores closed, the neighborhood taverns and saloons scattered among them stayed open. Men who frequented these places, furthermore, knew the areas well enough so that they were not likely to be surprised by muggers, especially since it would be common for them to travel in twos and threes back to their homes.

The residential neighborhoods themselves, filling in the vast areas between the radiating streetcar lines, were environments no more conducive to crime. That crime was not more commonly reported in these areas, it is true, may have been because police service was stretched thin there and residents did not find it convenient to make reports to police officers. But it seems reasonable to assume that these areas were in fact relatively crime-free, as the data show. These were neighborhoods in which there were always people around, young mothers or elderly grandparents, for instance, who were sitting on porches, standing in back yards, or staring out of windows. Potential burglars or muggers may have been well aware that someone was likely to notice anything suspicious or unusual. Everyday life in other parts of the city, like the boarding-house districts or even the disreputable near east side in general, may have been as animated, but perhaps people were doing more coming and going rather than lingering and watching. In any case, the fact that crime did not move to the outer parts of the city at the same rate as the population was the single most important factor in the steady decline of the overall crime rate during the 1870s and early 1880s.

If we assume, as many contemporaries did, that criminals were likely to live or be staying not far from where they committed their crimes, then the patterns of criminal residence should also have been weighted toward the central parts of the city, where most crimes occurred. A plotting of the residential addresses of offenders for serious crimes in 1879–81 (see Map V–1 again) shows this generally to have been the case. The fears of the respectable classes about the people in the lower-class and transient near east side were not entirely misplaced. The heaviest concentration of criminal residences, especially when one considers the distribution of the population as a whole, was in the corridor on the east side bounded by Brush and Russell streets, which ran parallel with and between Woodward Avenue and the Detroit & Milwaukee Railroad tracks. Furthermore, a full one-quarter of all offenders for serious crimes had no local address at all, and it was highly likely these people were putting up somewhere in the lower east side and near the depots in the many cheap lodging houses and saloon boarding houses. If the people who lived in the disreputable areas were not by nature criminally inclined, as many believed, most criminals in fact came from these areas.

Thus criminals in late nineteenth-century Detroit, as in today's city, were victimizing their own neighbors and acquaintances in run-down, lower-class areas; or they were invading and preying upon adjacent "high-rank" areas, such as commercial districts and upper-class residential enclaves.[12] The critical difference, however, is that today many urbanites have been able to put distances between themselves and high-crime sections of the city. In the Detroit of 1880, even the majority of elite residents had not been able to do this. "High-rank" areas were concentrated downtown. Differentiated as the city's social space was, it was not an environment in which people could truly isolate themselves from the tribulations and vicissitudes of urban living. Crime was a real threat and the police, therefore, a more vital and useful institution.

DETROIT AND THE AMERICAN EXPERIENCE

The emergence of a more orderly and less criminal Detroit in the latter part of the nineteenth century seems to have been part of a national urban trend. American cities saw much less day-to-day mob violence as the century wore on. Ethnic and racial group violence first appeared as a fact of urban life in the 1830s, then peaked in the 1850s amid the cacophonous rhetoric of Know-Nothingism. In the 1860s, however, it seemed to lessen, especially after the racial tensions fostered by the Civil War subsided. By the 1870s, intergroup street violence was clearly on the decline. New York's Orange Riot between Protestants and Catholics in 1871 was almost an urban anachronism. Not until the racial disorders of the World War I era, when blacks moved to northern cities in great numbers, would the United States experience another wave of urban intergroup violence comparable to that of the mid-nineteenth century.

There were, nonetheless, serious urban disorders over the last third of the nineteenth century, but as was the case in Detroit these were less pervasive and spontaneous and were less indicative of smaller such disturbances routinely taking place in city streets and neighborhoods. These were mostly labor disorders arising out of the inflammatory mix of striking workers and the forces sent by employers or civil authorities to deal with them. The new era was introduced spectacularly by the great railroad strikes of 1877. The transition from ethnic and racial street rioting to labor violence approximated the trend toward modern collective disorder Charles Tilly describes in the European context. "Collective violence," he writes, "like so many other features of social life, changed from a communal basis to an associational one." Violence erupted not from daily social relations but from the "deliberate confrontations of special-purpose associations."[13]

There is less certainty at this point that crime also diminished in American cities during the latter part of the nineteenth century. Real patterns of crime are hidden from the historian's view behind biased and incomplete sources. If not altogether an "accurate" record, statistics generated by the criminal justice system—police and courts—are the most useful sources that historians have. Systematic investigation of this data has only begun, and the studies done so far do not all cover the same years of the nineteenth century. The cities included—Buffalo, Boston, Salem, Columbus, and Oakland—do at least stand as a reasonably good cross-section of American urbanization. The results of this research show some common trends. Violent crime rose to high levels at various points during the 1850s, 1860s, and 1870s, with something of a national urban crime wave evident in the years just after the Civil War and attributed by many contemporaries to the war experience. On the whole, violent crime declined, especially after the late 1870s. Crimes of theft followed a similar pattern, though perhaps not such a volatile one. The rate of decrease was less precipitous and certain forms of theft may have increased slightly. In sum, it would seem safe to say that the incidence of all serious crime fell off in the late nineteenth-century city from the high levels of around the middle of the century.[14]

Historians have attributed the decline in street disorders and major crimes to a variety of causes. There is little doubt, for example, that the receptivity of the political structure affected the outbreak of mob violence. The inundation of American cities with a diverse immigrant population in the 1840s and 1850s had initially put a great strain on the democratic political process, thereby contributing to much of the disorder that befell the mid-century city. Election-day violence alone would have made the mid-nineteenth century a major era in urban violence. In time, however, ethnic groups were assimilated into the political structure, a process capped off by the emergence of the urban boss and his machine toward the end of the nineteenth century. Conflicts once resolved violently in the streets were now transferred to the conciliatory world of backroom politics. As Adrian Cook puts it, the city was perhaps more corrupt, but it was also less violent.[15]

A second and more overarching explanation offered for the steady decline in crime and disorder has to do with the process of industrialization. Despite the periodic recessions and depressions that marked the development of an industrial economy in the United States, the long-term effect was to raise the standard of living and broaden the horizons of economic opportunity. To a large degree, crime has always been a way for persons who cannot be employed by society to obtain some of the material rewards jobs would offer. In short, crime is meant to be remunerative. As industrialization proceeded in the nineteenth century it provided more and more people with the noncriminal economic opportunities they might earlier have been denied. In the process, crime declined.[16]

In a more general way, historians have argued that industrialization reduced crime and disorder by placing people into new and less abrasive relationships with each other. The preponderance of close face-to-face relationships that had once characterized urban life gave way in the mature industrial city to many more fleeting, impersonal contacts and secondary relationships, and a more formal style of doing business. Although the growing anonymity of the city enhanced the opportunities for criminals specializing in deception—"theft-by-trick" as Eric Monkkonen refers to it—nonetheless, far less likely to occur any more were those traditional crimes, such as assault and battery, that happen most frequently where relationships are on a highly personal level. Moreover, industrialization absorbed people into new work groups and associations, and this helped break down old cultural barriers that had created the tensions underlying group violence. Along with these changes in patterns of behavior came new standards of behavior. What was once tolerated was now prosecuted. This was a society where formal codes and a sense of order counted more than they did before. Industrialization, in effect, "civilized" urbanites.[17]

The difficulty with these interpretations of order and disorder in the nineteenth-century American city is that with a few exceptions they do not give to the city's changing physical environment the attention it merits. The social, political, and economic forces historians have emphasized to date were clearly at the heart of the undulating patterns of crime and disorder in the nineteenth-century city. There is no denying that, but the impact of these forces was to some degree regulated by the spatial context in which they operated, a spatial context undergoing rapid and profound change throughout the course of the nineteenth century.

So, even if ethnic and racial tensions were present in the city, deeply rooted and unrestrained by political assimilation or industrial accommodation, to be transformed into street violence they had to find a "battle zone"—points of physical contact between contending groups. Otherwise, the tensions would have had to release themselves in different ways and in different arenas. In the city of Detroit during the 1850s probably no group was more hostile to blacks than the Irish. Irish animosity toward blacks in the mid-nineteenth-century city is well documented, and stemmed from the competition for unskilled jobs and the insecurity of Irishmen who always found themselves relegated to the low end of the white social scale.[18] Yet street violence between blacks and the Irish in Detroit was no more common and conspicuous, perhaps even less so, than that between the Germans and the blacks, though the tension between those two groups appeared lower. The difference lay in the residential patterns of the two immigrant groups. Most Irishmen lived on Detroit's west side. Almost all the Germans lived on the east side, where they competed for space with the city's blacks, almost all of whom also lived there. The friction between the blacks and the Germans (and other whites on the east side, including the Irish) eventually manifested itself in the attacks on interracial houses of prostitution, as well as in the vicious rioting against blacks in 1863. In the meantime, both the Germans and the Irish in their neighborhoods on the urban periphery were sufficiently isolated from many potentially hostile native-born residents and transients that the chances for disorder arising out of anti-immigrant feelings were minimized. By the 1870s, whatever else was acting upon formerly violent groups to hold down street disorder, it was of more than a little consequence that the physical growth of the city brought these groups into less daily contact than had been the case before. Whites in working-class family neighborhoods now would have had to go out of their way to find blacks or rowdy houses of prostitution in order to express their hostility in violent behavior.

In the same way, the city's spatial development at least in part dictated the patterns of crime. The sorts of activity taking place and the number and kinds of people living in certain parts of the city had a bearing on the occurrence of crime above and beyond the degree to which criminally inclined persons lived in or frequented those areas. Criminals were likely to act where their victims or targets were most exposed and defenseless, and where they did not much risk being caught; in short, where the best opportunities presented themselves. In the growing and changing Detroit of the 1850s, the new central business district offered criminals one such environment, as did the emerging transient, low-amusement quarters. The introduction of a permanent police patrol into the heart of the city in 1865, however, undercut some of the features that had made these areas conducive to criminal behavior, and as a result the incidence of crime and ruffianism there was reduced by the 1870s.

This might all seem rather superficial to the student of current urban crime, who has come to expect more detailed, probing investigation of crime's spatial characteristics and determinants. Was there a link, for example, between urban crowding in nineteenth-century Detroit and aggressive behavior, as scholars have argued is the case in today's large cities?[19] Were such microenvironments as the boarding-house districts comparable to modern high-rise housing projects, where conditions particularly well suited to crime exist? That is, were buildings placed in such a way or their interiors constructed in such a manner as to encourage certain forms of criminal and disorderly behavior?[20] To answer these and similar questions historians would have to engage in spatial analyses of crime and disorder of a kind that would be extremely difficult given the sources at hand.

It might be more useful to explore in other cities the broader relationships between spatial development and the problem of

law and order in the manner done here for Detroit. Although
cities on the whole in the nineteenth century shared the
common experience of becoming more segregated in the
functional use of their land, spatial differentiation did not
always result in the same pattern. Moreover, if the distinction
between residential and nonresidential land use generally
increased, the patterns of residence themselves appear to have
varied. The ethnic clustering that occurred in Detroit at
mid-century was common in other western cities like Buffalo
and Milwaukee, but was less pronounced in eastern cities like
Boston and Philadelphia, suggesting a dichotomy between the
spatial development of older, mature cities in the mid-nineteenth century and that of young cities evolving rapidly from
almost nothing in these same years.[21]

The varieties of urban spatial development as they occurred
within a larger pattern common to all cities may help explain
why every city had a distinct experience in law and order even
as they all shared the breakdown of order in the middle years
of the nineteenth century and the return to order after that.
For example, no major city escaped significant mob violence in
the 1830–80 period as a result of the intense competition for
space among people, activities, and interests in an era of rapid
growth and unprecedented social change. Yet certain kinds of
violence were more prevalent in some cities than others.
Whorehouse rioting was common everywhere, but Detroit's
seems to have been a bit out of the ordinary in its amount and
intensity. On the other hand, Detroit had relatively little
ethno-religious disorder, certainly compared to a city like St.
Louis, which had four major native-immigrant riots in just the
one decade from 1844 to 1854. The antirailroad violence in
Detroit was similar to disorders in Philadelphia in the early
1840s, yet apparently few other cities experienced riotous
opposition to railroad tracks.[22] All these inconsistencies undoubtedly had some basis in differences among cities in spatial
develoment—who lived where and what went on where—just
as did the inconsistencies in the timing and logic of police
reform, as has already been suggested. There seems to be, in
other words, no way to overestimate the importance of the
city's geography to the problem of law and order. The ever-

changing features of its spatial arrangements were a critical component in the complex ordering of conditions that produced criminal and disorderly behavior and police reform in the nineteenth-century city.

NOTES

ABBREVIATIONS USED IN THE NOTES

N.B.: For a description of the important local records, see "A Note on the Detroit Sources," which follows the chapter notes.

BHC	Burton Historical Collection, Detroit Public Library
Mayor's Message	*Annual Message of the Mayor of the City of Detroit*
PD/CA	Police Department, Detroit City Archives, Burton Historical Collection
Procs. C.C.	*Journal of the Proceedings of the Common Council of the City of Detroit*
Rept. Water Comm.	*Annual Report of the Board of Water Commissioners to the Common Council of the City of Detroit*
Rept. Police Comm.	*Annual Report of the Board of Metropolitan Police Commissioners to the Common Council of the City of Detroit*
Rept. House of Correction	*Annual Report of the Inspectors of the Detroit House of Correction*

INTRODUCTION

1. David Harvey, *Social Justice and the City* (London: Edward Arnold, 1973), pp. 22–49.

2. John T. Cumbler, "City and Community: The Impact of Urban Forces on Working-Class Behavior," *Journal of Urban History* 3 (August 1977): 427–42. See also Theodore Hershberg's observation about the "ecological linkage" to urban attitudes and behavior in "The New Urban History: Toward an Interdisciplinary History of the City," ibid. 5 (November 1978): 13–14.

3. Sam Bass Warner, Jr., *The Private City: Philadelphia in Three Periods of its Growth* (Philadelphia: University of Pennsylvania Press, 1968), pp. 62, 125–57, 173. See also James F. Richardson, *Urban Police in the United States* (Port Washington: Kennikat, 1974), p. 63.

4. Bruce Laurie, "Fire Companies and Gangs in Southwark: The 1840s," in Allen F. Davis and Mark H. Haller, eds., *The Peoples of Philadelphia: A History of Ethnic Groups and Lower-Class Life, 1790–1940* (Philadelphia: Temple University Press, 1973), pp. 71–87.

5. Kevin Lynch, *The Image of the City* (Cambridge: MIT Press, 1960); Peter Gould and Rodney White, *Mental Maps* (Harmondsworth: Penguin, 1974); Gerald Suttles, *The Social Construction of Communities* (Chicago: University of Chicago Press, 1972).

6. Michael Frisch, *Town into City: Springfield, Massachusetts, and the Meaning of Community, 1840–1880* (Cambridge: Harvard University Press, 1972).

ONE: TROUBLE IN THE NEIGHBORHOODS

1. *Procs. C.C.* (1844–52), pp. 1272, 1330, 1511–12; *Detroit Free Press*, December 9, 1848, December 14, 1849, July 29, 1850; *Detroit Daily Advertiser*, December 14, 1849, February 12, 1850; Silas Farmer, *History of Detroit and Michigan, or the Metropolis Illustrated* (Detroit: Silas Farmer, 1884), p. 894. Occupations and residences of rioters from the city directory of 1850.

2. Floyd R. Dain, *Every House a Frontier: Detroit's Economic Progress, 1815–1825* (Detroit: Wayne University Press, 1956), pp. 1–92.

3. Almon E. Parkins, *The Historical Geography of Detroit* (Lansing: Michigan Historical Commission, 1918), pp. 170–226; John G. Clark, *The Grain Trade in the Old Northwest* (Urbana: University of Illinois Press, 1966), pp. 75–78.

4. John W. Reps, "Planning in the Wilderness: Detroit, 1805–1830," *Town Planning Review* 25 (January 1955): 240–50; John Farmer, *Map of the City of Detroit in the State of Michigan* (New York: C. B. & J. R. Graham, 1835).

5. Clarence M. Burton, comp., "Detroit City Directory of 1837 Arranged by Streets," bound typescript, BHC; Carl Abbott, "The Neighborhoods of New York, 1760–1775," *New York History* 55 (January 1974): 35–54; David Ward, *Cities and Immigrants: A Geography of Change in Nineteenth-Century America* (New York: Oxford University Press, 1971).

6. John C. Schneider, "Urbanization and the Maintenance of Order: Detroit, 1824–1847," *Michigan History* 60 (Fall 1976): 263–69; John Runcie, " 'Hunting the Nigs' in Philadelphia: The Race Riot of August, 1834," *Pennsylvania History* 39 (April 1972): 187–218.

7. *Detroit Journal and Advertiser*, July 10, 1835; *Free Press* (weekly edition), October 28, 1835; *Detroit Journal and Courier*, April 12, 1836; Robert E. Roberts, *Sketches and Reminiscences of the City of the Straits and Vicinity* (Detroit: Free Press, 1884), p. 101.

8. *Journal and Courier*, July 31, 1838; *Procs. C.C.* (1824–43), p. 462; *Advertiser*, March 5, 1840; Thomas W. Palmer, *Detroit in 1837* (Detroit: Burton Abstract and Title, 1922), p. 29.

9. Ethnic residential patterns gauged from surnames in Burton, "Detroit City Directory of 1837." For the Irish in Detroit during the 1830s and 1840s, JoEllen McNergney Vinyard, *The Irish on the Urban Frontier: Nineteenth-Century Detroit, 1850–1880* (New York: Arno Press, 1976), pp. 48–52.

10. David M. Johnson, "Crime Patterns in Philadelphia, 1840–1870," in Allen F. Davis and Mark H. Haller, eds., *The Peoples of Philadelphia: A History of Ethnic Groups and Lower-Class Life, 1790–1940* (Philadelphia: Temple University Press, 1973), pp. 97–101. On community attitudes toward the volunteer firemen in Detroit, John R. Williams to P. E. Demill, April 20, 1838, John R. Williams Papers, BHC; *Free Press*, January 18, 1847, December 18, 1850. On the fire companies of Boston and Philadelphia, Roger Lane, *Policing the City: Boston, 1822–1885* (Cambridge: Harvard University Press, 1967), pp. 33–34; Bruce Laurie, "Fire Companies and Gangs in Southwark: The 1840s," in Davis and Haller, *Peoples of Philadelphia*, pp. 71–87.

11. Charles S. Hathaway, *Our Firemen: A Record of the Faithful and Heroic Men Who Guard the Property and Lives in the City of Detroit* (Detroit: John F. Eby, 1894), pp. 73–75, 90; *Advertiser*, December 30, 1839. The four mayors were James A. Van Dyke (1847), John Patton (1858–59), Christian H. Buhl (1860–61), Hugh Moffat (1872–75).

12. *Free Press*, May 28, June 18, 1851, October 1, 1853, October 10, 1855; *Advertiser*, October 1, 1850, May 18, 1860; Robert E. Roberts, *Sketches of the City of Detroit, State of Michigan, Past and Present* (Detroit: R. F. Johnstone, 1855), p. 18; *Shove's Business Advertiser and Detroit*

Directory (Detroit: Free Press, 1852), pp. 53–54; C. C. Trowbridge to Alexander H. Sibley, January 10, 1852, A. H. Sibley Papers, BHC; U.S. Census Office, *Statistics of the United States in 1860* (Washington: Government Printing Office, 1865), p. xviii; Israel D. Andrews, "Report on Trade and Commerce of British North American Colonies and upon the Trade of the Great Lakes and Rivers," *Senate Executive Documents*, No. 112, 32nd Congress, First Session, 1853, pp. 97–135.

13. *Johnston's Detroit Directory and Business Advertiser* (Detroit: George E. Pomeroy, 1853), p. xiii.

14. Vinyard, *Irish on the Urban Frontier*, pp. 52–53.

15. Ibid., p. 103.

16. *Advertiser*, July 22, 1859.

17. Kathleen Neils Conzen, *Immigrant Milwaukee, 1836–1860: Accommodation and Community in a Frontier City* (Cambridge: Harvard University Press, 1976), pp. 64, 125, and *passim*.

18. Vinyard, *Irish on the Urban Frontier*, pp. 62, 87–88; Jon M. Kingdale, "The 'Poor Man's Club': Social Functions of the Urban Working-Class Saloon," *American Quarterly* 25 (October 1973): 477–89; Bruce Laurie, " 'Nothing on Compulsion': Life Styles of Philadelphia Artisans, 1820–1850," *Labor History* 15 (Summer 1974): 346–47; Conzen, *Immigrant Milwaukee*, pp. 156–58.

19. Andrew M. Greeley, *Why Can't They Be Like Us?: America's White Ethnic Groups* (New York: E. P. Dutton, 1971), pp. 95–105, 155; Gerald Suttles, *The Social Construction of Communities* (Chicago: University of Chicago Press, 1972), pp. 21–23. See also, Suzanne Keller, *The Urban Neighborhood: A Sociological Perspective* (New York: Random House, 1968), pp. 51–53.

20. *Advertiser*, October 23, November 18, 1841; *Procs. C.C.* (1824–43), pp. 517–8, 684–85, 717, 722–24, 726, 728, 730; *Elizabeth Welch* v. *Stowell et al.* (1846), 2 Douglass 332.

21. William W. Sanger, *The History of Prostitution: Its Extent, Causes and Effects Throughout the World*, reprint ed. (New York: Eugenics, 1939), pp. 549–74.

22. Spatial patterns of prostitution pieced together from references in *Free Press*, January 29, September 11, 1852, November 29, 1853, November 25, 1854, July 6–7, 1855, June 9–10, 21, August 4, 7–8, 1857, May 7, June 4, July 11, 24, 27, August 13, 26, 1858, April 7, May 26, July 20, 23, August 17, 23–24, October 13, November 1, 1859; *Advertiser*, July 6, 10, 1855, July 1, 1856, February 5, June 22–23, July 13, August 22, November 24, 1857, July 12–13, 1858, May 3, 1859.

school crisis of 1853 is well described in Vinyard, *Irish on the ~ Frontier,* pp. 205–35; Ronald P. Formisano, *The Birth of Mass Political Parties: Michigan, 1827–1861* (Princeton: Princeton University Press, 1971), pp. 222–27.

24. Formisano, *Birth of Mass Parties,* pp. 229–38; *Free Press,* February 24, 1855.

25. *Advertiser,* May 10, 1856; *Free Press,* December 23, 1853, January 5, 1854, October 21, 1855, April 13, May 9–10, 1856; John J. Flinn and John E. Wilkie, *History of the Chicago Police* (Chicago: Police Book Fund, 1887), pp. 70–79; James F. Richardson, *The New York Police: From Colonial Times to 1901* (New York: Oxford University Press, 1970), p. 110.

26. *Advertiser,* June 7, 1858; *Free Press,* May 14, 30, June 2, 1858.

27. *Rept. Water Comm.* (1857), pp. 53–54; *Charles F. Clark's Annual Directory of the Inhabitants, Incorporated Companies, Business Firms, etc., of the City of Detroit* (Detroit: Charles F. Clark, 1862), p. 328.

28. *Procs. C.C.* (1854), pp. 122, 124–25, 133; *Procs. C.C.* (1857), pp. 66–67; *Procs. C.C.* (1858), p. 70. Occupations and residences of petitioners from the city directories of 1852 and 1857.

29. *Procs. C.C.* (1857), pp. 66–67; *Procs. C.C.* (1858), pp. 87, 92–93; *Procs. C.C.* (1859), pp. 144–45.

30. *Advertiser,* July 13, 1857; *Free Press,* July 12, 14, 1857.

31. *Free Press,* May 10, 1856. The *Free Press* claimed to have evidence from a local madam that Hyde refused to act on behalf of antivice interests because he had a pecuniary stake in some of the east side brothels. *Free Press,* June 28, 30, 1857.

32. Names of aldermen listed in Farmer, *History of Detroit,* pp. 143–44. On German support for the Democrats, Formisano, *Birth of Mass Political Parties,* pp. 301–2.

33. Lane, *Policing the City,* p. 24; Maximilian I. Reichard, "Origins of the Urban Police: Freedom and Order in Antebellum St. Louis" (Ph.D. diss., Washington University, 1975), p. 179; John C. Schneider, "Riot and Reaction in St. Louis, 1854–1856," *Missouri Historical Review* 68 (January 1974): 176; Constance M. Green, *The Secret City: A History of Race Relations in the Nation's Capital* (Princeton: Princeton University Press, 1967), p. 36; Philip D. Jordan, *Frontier Law and Order: Ten Essays* (Lincoln: University of Nebraska Press, 1970), pp. 118, 126.

34. *Detroit Journal and Michigan Advertiser,* September 10, 1834; *Free Press,* September 6, 27, 1847, January 20, 1852.

35. For this and the following discussions of the brothel violence, *Free Press,* July 6–7, 1855, June 14, 25, 1856, June 21, 23, August 4,

1857, June 4, 1858, May 3, July 20, 23, 1859; *Advertiser,* July 6, 10, 1855, May 28, July 1, 1856, June 22–23, November 24, 1857, May 3, July 22, 1859. On the anti-abolition disorders of the 1830s, Leonard L. Richards, *"Gentlemen of Property and Standing:" Anti-Abolition Mobs in Jacksonian America* (New York: Oxford University Press, 1970).

36. *Detroit Daily Tribune,* June 22, 1857; *Procs. C.C.* (1858), pp. 87, 92–93.

37. *Free Press,* July 3, 1857.

38. Arrestees reported in *Free Press,* July 7, 1855, August 16, 1857; *Advertiser,* May 28, 1856; occupations and residences from the city directories of 1856 and 1857.

39. *Free Press,* July 8, 1855, June 23, 1857, June 4, 1858; *Advertiser,* July 6, 10, 1855.

40. *Free Press,* July 18, 1857, July 20, 23, 1859; *Advertiser,* July 22, 1859.

41. *Free Press,* August 23–24, October 13, 1859, May 6, 1860, January 23–24, 30, 1864, October 6, 1865.

42. Ibid., July 4, 1857.

43. *Advertiser,* July 5, 1856, May 3, 1859; *Free Press,* May 3, 1859.

44. *Free Press,* August 16, 18–19, 26, 1857.

TWO: THE NEW DOWNTOWN

1. *Shove's Business Advertiser and Detroit Directory* (Detroit: Free Press, 1852), pp. 53–54; *Rept. Water Comm.* (1862), p. 75; *Free Press,* April 10, July 20, 1849, April 22, 1850, May 24, December 10, 1851, August 27, 1854.

2. *Free Press,* May 10–11, 1848, April 29, 1850; Robert E. Roberts, *Sketches of the City of Detroit, State of Michigan, Past and Present* (Detroit: R. F. Johnstone, 1855), p. 18.

3. Dr. Morse Stewart to Isabella G. Duffield, June 23, 1851, Morse Stewart Papers, BHC; *Free Press,* September 6, 1851, May 11, 1854, May 1, 1855, May 31, 1861.

4. *Procs. C.C.* (1844–52), pp. 1095, 1097; *Free Press,* March 5, 12, April 4, 1846, June 12, 1848; W. Hawkins Ferry, *The Buildings of Detroit* (Detroit: Wayne State University Press, 1968), p. 35.

5. *Free Press,* April 10, 1848, April 7, 1849; *Shove's Business Advertiser,* pp. 54–55; John G. Clark, *The Grain Trade in the Old Northwest* (Urbana: University of Illinois Press, 1966), pp. 249–50; David Ward, *Cities and Immigrants: A Geography of Change in Nineteenth-Century America* (New York: Oxford University Press, 1971), pp. 89–92.

6. *Map of Detroit* (Detroit: n.p., 1849?). Silas Farmer credits this map to Henry Hart, 1853. Silas Farmer, *History of Detroit and Michi-*

gan, or the *Metropolis Illustrated* (Detroit: Silas Farmer, 1884), p. 374.

7. Stephan Thernstrom and Peter R. Knights, "Men in Motion: Some Data and Speculations about Urban Population Mobility in Nineteenth-Century America," *Journal of Interdisciplinary History* 1 (Autumn 1970): 24–27; Michael B. Katz, Michael J. Doucet, and Mark J. Stern, "Migration and the Social Order in Erie County, New York, 1855," ibid. 8 (Spring 1978): 669–701.

8. John Modell and Tamara Hareven, "Urbanization and the Malleable Household: An Examination of Boarding and Lodging in American Families," *Journal of Marriage and the Family* 35 (August 1973): 473.

9. Number and location by ward of boarding houses from *Rept. Water Comm.* (1854), p. 62; *Rept. Water Comm.* (1857), pp. 53–54; *Rept. Water Comm.* (1862), pp. 71–72; *Rept. Water Comm.* (1865), pp. 32–33; *Rept. Water Comm.* (1869), pp. 51–52.

10. *Johnston's Detroit Directory and Business Advertiser* (Detroit: George E. Pomeroy, 1853), p. xiv; Michigan Dept. of State, *Census and Statistics of the State of Michigan* (Lansing: George W. Peck, 1854), pp. 367–74. Also, Roberts, *Sketches,* pp. 30–31.

11. I am indebted to Ned Polsky, "Of Pool Playing and Poolrooms," in Gregory P. Stone, ed., *Games, Sport, and Power* (New Brunswick, N.J.: E. P. Dutton, 1972), pp. 44–47, for useful ideas about the "bachelor subculture," as well as for the term itself.

12. *Detroit Daily Post,* August 23, 1871. The number of saloons in the city was included in the reports of the Board of Water Commissioners (see note 9).

13. Polsky, "Of Pool Playing and Poolrooms," pp. 47–48; *Free Press,* April 13, 1859; *Post,* July 23, 1866; *Charles F. Clark's Annual Directory of the Inhabitants, Incorporated Companies, Business Firms, etc., of the City of Detroit* (Detroit: Charles F. Clark, 1862), p. 325.

14. Paul Jacobson, *American Marriage and Divorce* (New York: Rinehart, 1959), pp. 35–36, 62; Michigan Dept. of State, *Annual Report of the Secretary of State on the Registration of Births and Deaths, Marriages and Divorces in Michigan* (Lansing: Wynkoop, Hallenbeck, Crawford, 1915), p. 64.

15. *Free Press,* July 22, 1850; *Shove's Business Advertiser,* p. 59.

16. Vice patterns pieced together from references in *Free Press,* January 24, February 19, May 25, 1860, February 6, March 7, April 20, May 13, June 4, 1862, January 30, February 19, 22–23, April 14, May 29, 1863, January 6–8, 23–24, April 12, July 27, December 20, 1864, January 20, February 20, August 23–24, 1865; *Advertiser,* January 30, May 7, 24, 1860, January 22, 1861, January 6, November 22, 1864; *Post,* April 24, 1866, June 27, 1867. Exact locations of billiard

halls, boarding houses, and saloons in *Clark's Directory*, pp. 325–26, 349–51. The boarding houses and saloons listed in the directory clearly do not include all those in the city. Likely missing are most of the smaller or least respectable places.

17. *Free Press*, June 23, 1857, July 20, 23, 1859; *Advertiser*, July 22, 1859. Philadelphia's and Chicago's vice areas in the 1860s were also downtown, near the boarding houses. See David R. Johnson, *Policing the Urban Underworld: The Impact of Crime on the Development of the American Police, 1800–1887* (Philadelphia: Temple University Press, 1979), p. 152.

18. Robert E. Park and Ernest W. Burgess, *The City* (Chicago: University of Chicago Press, 1925), pp. 76–77; Walter C. Reckless, *Vice in Chicago* (Chicago: University of Chicago Press, 1933), pp. 164–65.

19. *Free Press*, May 29, 1863, January 20, August 23, 1865; *Post*, April 24, 1866, June 27, 1867; Farmer, *History of Detroit*, p. 928.

20. David M. Katzman, *Before the Ghetto: Black Detroit in the Nineteenth Century* (Urbana: University of Illinois Press, 1973), pp. 25–27; Gerald D. Suttles, *The Social Construction of Communities* (Chicago: University of Chicago Press, 1972), p. 239.

21. Wealthy residential patterns, 1840–60, determined by plotting the addresses (from the city directories of 1845 and 1861) of those listed as Detroit's wealthiest men in Alexandra McCoy, "Political Affiliations of American Economic Elites: Wayne County, Michigan, 1844, 1860, as a Test Case" (Ph.D. diss., Wayne State University, 1965), pp. 56–61, 71–82.

22. See Edward Pessen, *Riches, Class, and Power Before the Civil War* (Lexington, Mass.: D. C. Heath, 1973), pp. 169–204. Also, Kathleen Neils Conzen, *Immigrant Milwaukee, 1836–1860: Accommodation and Community in a Frontier City* (Cambridge: Harvard University Press, 1976), p. 147.

23. *Free Press*, September 20, 1856; Ferry, *Buildings of Detroit*, pp. 51–58.

24. *Free Press*, September 7, December 7, 9, 1855, April 9, 1863; Ferry, *Buildings of Detroit*, pp. 47–48. Pew-holders listed in *Free Press*, November 20, 1855.

25. *Advertiser*, September 2, 1847, March 27, 1849. Also, *Free Press*, October 19, 1847, April 8, 25, 1853.

26. Farmer, *History of Detroit*, p. 786; *Advertiser*, March 21, 1854, July 12, 1859; *Free Press*, February 25, 1854, June 27–28, 1862, January 20, 1866.

27. *Free Press*, June 27, August 7, 1856; Farmer, *History of Detroit*, p. 787–92.

28. List of Board of Trade members in *Free Press*, February 27, 1864; addresses from the city directories of 1863 and 1864.

29. Kirk Jeffrey, "The Family as Utopian Retreat from the City: The Nineteenth-Century Contribution," *Soundings* 55 (Spring 1972): 21–22; Clifford Clark, Jr., "Domestic Architecture as an Index to Social History: The Romantic Revival and the Cult of Domesticity in America, 1840–1870," *Journal of Interdisciplinary History* 7 (Summer 1976): 40.

30. *Free Press*, February 13, 1867; also, February 10, 1866.

31. Michael B. Katz, *The People of Hamilton, Canada West: Family and Class in a Mid-Nineteenth-Century City* (Cambridge: Harvard University Press, 1975), pp. 36–37, 264–65.

32. Egon Bittner, "The Police on Skid Row: A Study of Peace Keeping," *American Sociological Review* 32 (October 1967): 699–715; Harvey Zorbaugh, *The Gold Coast and the Slum: A Sociological Study of Chicago's Near North Side* (Chicago: University of Chicago Press, 1929), pp. 69, 86.

33. Clark, "Domestic Architecture," pp. 51–52.

34. *Procs. C.C.* (1861), p. 13; *Procs. C.C.* (1862), p. 126; *Procs. C.C.* (1866), pp. 181–84; *Advertiser*, October 31, 1854; *Free Press*, August 27, September 20, 1865.

THREE: THE CRISIS DOWNTOWN

1. George A. Ketcham, "Municipal Police Reform: A Comparative Study of Law Enforcement in Cincinnati, Chicago, New Orleans, New York, and St. Louis, 1844–1877" (Ph.D. diss., University of Missouri, 1967); Roger Lane, *Policing the City: Boston, 1822–1885* (Cambridge: Harvard University Press, 1967); James F. Richardson, *The New York Police: Colonial Times to 1901* (New York: Oxford University Press, 1970).

2. Michael Feldberg, "Urbanization as a Cause of Violence: Philadelphia as a Test Case," in Allen F. Davis and Mark H. Haller, eds., *The Peoples of Philadelphia: A History of Ethnic Groups and Lower-Class Life, 1790–1940* (Philadelphia: Temple University Press, 1973), pp. 53–69; John K. Alexander, "City of Brotherly Fear: The Poor in Late-Eighteenth-Century Philadelphia," in Kenneth Jackson and Stanley K. Schultz, eds., *Cities in American History* (New York: Knopf, 1972), pp. 79–97; Leonard L. Richards, *"Gentlemen of Property and Standing:" Anti-Abolition Mobs in Jacksonian America* (New York: Oxford University Press, 1970); Richard Hofstadter and Michael Wallace, eds., *American Violence: A Documentary History* (New York: Random House, 1970), p. 11.

3. Allan E. Levett, "Centralization of the City Police in the Nineteenth-Century United States" (Ph.D. diss., University of Michigan, 1974); Maximilian I. Reichard, "The Origins of Urban Police: Freedom and Order in Ante-Bellum St. Louis" (Ph.D. diss., Washington University, 1975); Sidney Harring, "The Development of the Police Institution in the United States," *Crime and Social Justice* 5 (Spring–Summer 1976): 54–59; Alan Dawley, *Class and Community: The Industrial Revolution in Lynn* (Cambridge: Harvard University Press, 1976), pp. 104–13; Wilbur R. Miller, Jr., *Cops and Bobbies: Police Authority in New York and London, 1830–1870* (Chicago: University of Chicago Press, 1977).

4. John C. Schneider, "Urbanization and the Maintenance of Order: Detroit, 1824–1847," *Michigan History* 60 (Fall 1976): 266–67.

5. *Advertiser,* April 8, 1852, June 30, 1854; *Free Press,* December 8, 1854; *Procs. C.C.* (1863), pp. 228–29.

6. *Free Press,* September 5, 1848, December 10, 1850, March 15, 1852, May 25, 1853, February 5, July 12, October 3, 6, 1854, July 16, 22, December 7, 1856, January 31, May 15, July 7, October 27, 1857.

7. *Advertiser,* June 28, 1854; *Free Press,* June 22, 1855. Also, *Advertiser,* September 4, 27–28, 1848, June 30, November 13, December 8, 1854; *Free Press,* September 28, 1848, March 18, 1850, December 10, 1851, February 24, 1852, June 27, 30, July 1–2, 4, November 23, December 29, 1854, May 1, June 19, 1855, July 8, 1857, January 21, May 26, 1858, January 30, February 6, 8, March 11, 1859, January 30, July 28, August 30, December 18, 1863, February 24, December 15, 1864.

8. Charles Hirschfield, *The Great Railroad Conspiracy: The Social History of a Railroad War* (East Lansing: Michigan State College Press, 1953), pp. 1–55; *Free Press,* November 20, 1850, April 21, May 22, 1851; *Procs. C.C.* (1844–52), p. 1610; James A. Van Dyke, *Argument in the Railroad Conspiracy Case, Entitled the People of Michigan* vs. *Abel F. Fitch and Others* (Detroit: Duncklee, Wales, 1851), pp. 5–6.

9. *Free Press,* January 26, 1850, November 23, 1854, March 18, August 30, 1864; *Advertiser,* May 22, 1860; *Detroit Advertiser and Tribune,* April 26, 1864. Also, *Free Press,* November 24, 1853, June 27, July 1–2, October 26, 1854, November 30, December 8, 1864; *Advertiser,* July 11, November 24, 1854; *Procs. C.C.* (1863), p. 229.

10. Index of Suspicious Places and Record of Complaints (1865–68), pp. 71–136, PD/CA.

11. David R. Johnson, "Crime Patterns in Philadehia, 1840–1870," in Davis and Haller, *Peoples of Philadelphia,* pp. 90–96; Reichard, "Origins of Urban Police," pp. 244, 279–80.

12. Michigan Dept. of State, *Census and Statistics of the State of*

Michigan (Lansing: George W. Peck, 1854), pp. 367–74; U.S. Census Office, *Statistics of the Population of the United States* (Washington: Government Printing Office, 1872), p. 176. For the pressure of commercial "facilities" on residential space downtown, *Rept. Water Comm.* (1857), p. 77; *Rept. Water Comm.* (1863), p. 59; *Rept. Water Comm.* (1871), p. 36.

13. Clarence M. Burton, *History of Detroit, 1780–1850: Financial and Commercial* (Detroit: n.p., 1917), p. 167.

14. *Free Press*, May 28, 1857; *Procs. C.C.* (1864), pp. 251, 261–62.

15. *Free Press*, October 17, 1849.

16. *Procs. C.C.* (1855), p. 34; *Free Press*, July 4, 1854; *Advertiser*, July 3, 1854.

17. *Free Press*, November 3–4, 11, 21, December 3, 8, 19–20, 23, 1854, March 7–8, 11, 1856; *Advertiser*, November 22, 24, 1854, March 7, 1856; *Procs. C.C.* (1856), pp. 22, 159.

18. *Free Press*, March 7, 1856. Also, *Advertiser*, March 7, 1856.

19. *Free Press*, December 23, 1854, March 7, 1856; *Advertiser*, July 12, 1854; Silas Farmer, *History of Detroit, and Michigan, or the Metropolis Illustrated* (Detroit: Silas Farmer, 1884), p. 161.

20. *Free Press*, November 15, 1854; *Advertiser*, November 13, 24, 1854.

21. *Free Press*, December 20, 1857.

22. Ibid., May 27–28, 1858, January 29, February 22, 24, 1859; *Advertiser*, May 27, 1858, February 1, 1859.

23. *Free Press*, February 24, 1859.

24. Ibid., May 27–28, 1858, January 29, February 22, 24, April 2, May 7, August 10, 1859, March 7, 1860.

25. Ibid., November 23, 1859.

26. *Johnston's Detroit City Directory and Advertising Gazeteer of Michigan* (Detroit: Fisher, Fleming, 1857), pp. 94–95; *Free Press*, September 17, 1854, May 3, 1855, March 12, 1856, January 28, October 29, 1858, January 4, 1859, July 14, 1860, April 17, July 6, 1861; *Advertiser*, May 4, 26, 1855; *Procs. C.C.* (1862), pp. 60, 150–51.

27. *Free Press*, August 26, 1858, July 20, 1859.

28. Farmer, *History of Detroit*, pp. 305–8; *Free Press*, May 11, 28, 1861.

29. *Free Press*, July 20, August 13, 26–27, 1858, April 16, 1859; *Advertiser*, May 21, 1860; *Procs. C.C.* (1859), p. 304; *Procs. C.C.* (1861), p. 13; *Procs. C.C.* (1862), pp. 126, 176–77, 194, 200. Also, *Free Press*, July 24, 1858, January 23, 30, May 29, 1863.

30. *Advertiser*, November 13, 1854; *Free Press*, October 26, 1854, February 27, 1859, February 24, 1864; *Procs. C.C.* (1862), pp. 176–77. Also, *Advertiser*, November 24, 1854.

31. *Free Press,* August 23, 1865.

32. Ibid., May 29, 1863.

33. Ibid., August 12, 1845. See Schneider, "Urbanization and the Maintenance of Order," pp. 269–70.

34. *Procs. C.C.* (1844–52), pp. 1571, 1645–46.

35. *Advertiser,* November 14, 1854, February 28, 1863; *Free Press,* July 23, August 4, 1854, February 25, July 23, 1859, August 10–12, 1863, March 26, 1865; *Procs. C.C.* (1865), pp. 226–27. Jail data reported in *Free Press,* November 18, 1847, May 16, 1848, May 27, November 16, 1854, November 2, December 1, 1863, January 1, February 2, March 3, April 1, May 2, June 1, July 1, August 1, September 1, October 2, 1864.

36. *Free Press,* July 16–17, 22, August 24, December 31, 1862, February 4, 18, 21, 25, 1863; *Advertiser and Tribune,* July 16, 1862; Eugene C. Murdock, *Patriotism Limited, 1862–1865: The Civil War Draft and Bounty System* (Kent: Kent State University Press, 1967), pp. 7–9; John Robertson, *Michigan in the War* (Lansing: W. S. George, 1880), pp. 23–38.

37. *Free Press,* June 28, 1861, December 2, 24–25, 1862, February 13, 15–16, 19–21, 1863; Justin E. Walsh, "Radically and Thoroughly Democratic: Wilbur F. Storey and the Detroit *Free Press,* 1853 to 1861," *Michigan History* 47 (September 1963): 193–225; V. Jacque Voegeli, *Free But Not Equal: The Midwest and the Negro during the Civil War* (Chicago: University of Chicago Press, 1967), p. 55.

38. *Free Press,* September 7, 1862.

39. Ibid., February 27, March 1, 1863; *Detroit Journal,* May 30, 1888.

40. *Free Press,* March 6–7, 1863; *Advertiser and Tribune,* March 7, 1863; Thomas Cooley, comp., *The Compiled Laws of the State of Michigan,* 2 vols. (Lansing: Hosmer & Kerr, 1857), 2:1506.

41. *Free Press,* March 7–8, 1863; *Advertiser and Tribune,* March 7, 1863; *A Thrilling Narrative from the Lips of the Sufferers of the Late Detroit Riot, March 6, 1863, with the Hair Breadth Escape of Men, Women and Children, and Destruction of Colored Men's Property, Not Less than $15,000,* reprint ed. (Hattiesburg, Miss.: Charles F. Heartman, 1945), pp. 2–13; Adrian Cook, *Armies of the Street: The New York Draft Riots of 1863* (Lexington: University of Kentucky Press, 1974), p. 78.

42. *Advertiser and Tribune,* March 9, 1863; *Free Press,* March 7–8, 14, 24–28, April 15, 17, May 27, 29, 31, June 18, 1863; *A Thrilling Narrative,* pp. 3, 6, 10–11.

43. *Free Press,* March 8, 1863; *Advertiser and Tribune,* March 7, 1863.

44. *Free Press,* March 7–8, April 1, 1863; *Advertiser and Tribune,*

March 7, 10, 1863; *Procs. C.C.* (1863), p. 245.

45. Michael Feldberg, *The Philadelphia Riots of 1844: A Study in Ethnic Conflict* (Westport, Conn.: Greenwood, 1975), pp. 114, 120, 123; John C. Schneider, "Riot and Reaction in St. Louis, 1854–1856," *Missouri Historical Review* 68 (January 1974): 179.

46. *Free Press*, March 7–8, 1863; *Advertiser and Tribune*, March 9, 12, 1863. Occupations of meeting participants from the city directory of 1863.

47. *Procs. C.C.* (1863), pp. 242, 245, 250.

48. *Free Press*, October 26, 31, November 1, 5, 7, December 14, 17, 28, 1864; *Advertiser and Tribune*, November 1, 5, 1864; *Procs. C.C.* (1865), pp. 190–93; Minutes of the Board of Police Commissioners Meetings (1864), October 27–28, November 15, PD/CA.

49. *Free Press*, November 22–23, December 6, 1864, January 10, 1865; *Advertiser and Tribune*, November 17, 24, December 14, 1864, January 24, February 3, 9, 1865; Minutes of the Board of Police Commissioners Meetings (1864), November 2–3, PD/CA.

50. *Free Press*, June 22, 1850, November 24, December 15, 1852, April 8, June 3, 1853, October 3, 18, 1854, October 27, November 24, 26–27, December 3–4, 1857, October 1, 1859, October 10, 1860, July 31, 1861; *Advertiser*, November 20, 1854, December 11, 1857; *Rept. House of Correction* (1872), pp. 98–111.

51. *Free Press*, December 6, 1855, April 25, May 2, June 4, 1856, April 8, May 27, October 9, 1857, January 26, May 23, September 16, November 24, 1858, January 28, May 25, 1859, April 15, October 12, November 14, 25, 1860, January 8, 1863; *Advertiser*, October 20, 1860.

52. Paul Kleppner, *The Cross of Culture: A Social Analysis of Midwestern Politics, 1850–1900* (New York: Free Press, 1970), p. 75.

53. *Procs. C.C.* (1860), pp. 121–2; *Procs. C.C.* (1862), p. 2; *Free Press*, October 27, 1859, January 8, 24, 1861, January 25, 1862; *Acts of the Legislature of the State of Michigan Passed at the Regular and Extra Sessions of 1861* (Lansing: John A. Kerr, 1861), pp. 199–203.

54. *Procs. C.C.* (1863), pp. 219, 228–30; *Advertiser and Tribune*, February 16, 1863.

55. *Advertiser and Tribune*, March 9, 1863, April 30, 1864; *Free Press*, July 23, August 12, 1863; *Procs. C.C.* (1863), pp. 251, 253; *Procs. C.C.* (1864), pp. 16, 106; *Procs. C.C.* (1865), p. 10.

56. *Advertiser and Tribune*, November 10, 1864; *Free Press*, January 14, 1865.

57. *Free Press*, January 19, 1865; Farmer, *History of Detroit*, p. 204; *Rept. House of Correction* (1863), pp. 11–12; *Rept. House of Correction* (1864), p. 7.

58. _Advertiser and Tribune,_ April 7, 1864; _Free Press,_ January 26, 1865.

59. _Free Press,_ November 23–24, 1864, January 31, February 11, 1865; _Advertiser and Tribune,_ January 12, 1865; _Procs. C.C._ (1865), pp. 225–27. Also, _Journal of the House of Representatives of the State of Michigan, 1865_ (Lansing: John A. Kerr, 1865), pp. 383–84.

60. _Free Press,_ January 14, 1865.

61. Ibid., June 9, 1865; _Procs. C.C._ (1866), p. 55.

62. _Free Press,_ February 21, March 2, 1865.

63. Reichard, "Origins of Urban Police," pp. 72–89, 151–54; Miller, _Cops and Bobbies,_ pp. 141–44.

FOUR: THE PROFESSIONAL POLICE AND THE CITY

1. Victor S. Clark, _History of Manufactures in the United States, 1860–1914_ (Washington: Carnegie Institute of Washington, 1928), p. 131; Almon E. Parkins, _The Historical Geography of Detroit_ (Lansing: Michigan Historical Commission, 1918), pp. 287–301; Thomas S. Beals, _The Commercial, Industrial, and Transportation Interests of the City of Detroit_ (Washington: Government Printing Office, 1882), pp. 10–14.

2. Silas Farmer, _Guide Map of the City of Detroit_ (Detroit: Silas Farmer, 1863), and _Guide Map of the City of Detroit_ (Detroit: Silas Farmer, 1886). On late nineteenth-century urban spatial development, the classic study is Sam Bass Warner, Jr., _Streetcar Suburbs: The Process of Growth in Boston, 1870–1900_ (Cambridge: Harvard University Press, 1962).

3. _Free Press,_ May 20, 1862, August 4, 1863; Silas Farmer, _Map and Manual of the City of Detroit_ (Detroit: Silas Farmer, 1872), pp. 27–31; Graeme O'Geran, _A History of the Detroit Street Railways_ (Detroit: Conover Press, 1931), pp. 25–26.

4. _Free Press,_ September 25, October 13, November 2, 15, 1863, November 3, 1867, April 7, 1868, May 7, 14, 1870, July 17, 1873, June 18, 28, 1876; _Advertiser and Tribune,_ October 26, 1864; Michigan Dept. of State, _Statistics of the State of Michigan_ (Lansing: John A. Kerr, 1861), p. 301; U.S. Census Office, _Statistics of the Population of the United States_ (Washington: Government Printing Office, 1872), pp. 600–601; Silas Farmer, _History of Detroit and Michigan, or the Metropolis Illustrated_ (Detroit: Silas Farmer, 1884), p. 376.

5. Elite residential patterns in the 1870s revealed in the listing of the addresses of Detroit's "first class people" in B. E. Fanning, _Pocket or Carriage Directory of the City of Detroit_ (Detroit: Machris, 1876).

6. _Free Press,_ September 8, 15, 1864, February 10, April 25, 1866,

November 21, 1869; *Post,* July 16, 1866; *Rept. Water Comm.* (1872), p. 10; David M. Katzman, *Before the Ghetto: Black Detroit in the Nineteenth Century* (Urbana: University of Illinois Press, 1973), pp. 71–75.

7. *Free Press,* January 17, November 21, 1869; *Post,* March 20, 1876.

8. *Free Press,* March 17, 1868, November 21, 1869 (an issue with a superbly detailed description of the city); Farmer, *History of Detroit,* pp. 770–73; Richard Edwards, *Industries of Michigan, City of Detroit: Historical and Descriptive Review* (New York: Historical Publications, 1880), p. 58.

9. *Free Press,* March 15, 1869, July 4, 1871; W. Hawkins Ferry, *The Buildings of Detroit* (Detroit: Wayne State University Press, 1968), pp. 77–79.

10. Farmer, *History of Detroit,* pp. 802–36; Michigan Dept. of State, *Census of the State of Michigan* (Lansing: W. S. George, 1875), p. 384. Also deemphasizing the role of the streetcar in outward residential growth, Edward K. Muller and Paul A. Groves, "The Changing Location of the Clothing Industry: A Link to the Social Geography of Baltimore in the Nineteenth Century," *Maryland Historical Magazine* 71 (Fall 1976): 403–20.

11. Locations of boarding houses from *Detroit City Directory* (Detroit: Free Press, 1880), pp. 891–92. Again, this is clearly not an exhaustive list.

12. *Free Press,* October 21, 1879; Albert B. Wolfe, *The Lodging House Problem in Boston* (Boston: Houghton, Mifflin, 1906), pp. 38–51.

13. Lists of saloons and billiard halls (not exhaustive, once again) in *J. W. Weeks & Co.'s Annual Directory of Detroit* (Detroit: J. W. Weeks, 1875), pp. 629, 667–70. Vice patterns derived from a plotting of the addresses of all the prostitutes arrested by the police (for all crimes) in 1879 and 1880. General Arrest Register, vol. 7 (1878–80), vol. 8 (1880–81), PD/CA. Also on vice areas, *Post,* April 2, 1872; *Detroit Post and Tribune,* February 16, 1880; *Free Press,* July 25, 1880; Katzman, *Before the Ghetto,* pp. 74, 172–73.

14. In the 1880s, a new police superintendent decided to clean out the Potomac Quarter. He succeeded in closing many houses, but in the process forced some prostitutes to solicit in the streets of the nearby central business district. *Rept. Police Comm.* (1883), pp. 29–30; Edwin F. Conely Scrapbook. vol. 2 (Police Matters, 1882), Michigan Historical Collections, Ann Arbor.

15. *Post,* April 24, 1866; *Free Press,* July 25, 1880; *Detroit Evening News,* July 30, 1875.

16. *News,* August 3, 1875; *Free Press,* August 29, 1876. Also, *Post,*

June 27, 1867, July 16, 1873; *Free Press,* June 28, 1878.

17. *Mayor's Message* (1876), p. 16; Alfred Russell to Gov. C. M. Croswell, February 4, 1877, Box 64, Recs. Exec. Office, Michigan State Archives, Lansing; Minutes of the Board of Metropolitan Police Commissioners Meetings, vol. 1 (1865–75): 320–21, PD/CA. Police commissioners listed in Farmer, *History of Detroit,* p. 205; occupations and business addresses from the various city directories, 1865–80.

18. Personnel requirements in *Manual for the Government of the Police Force of the City of Detroit* (Detroit: Advertiser and Tribune, 1865), pp. 3–4. Police wage scale, 1865–77, in Minutes of the Board of Metropolitan Police Commissioners Meetings, vol. 2 (1875–83): 118–21, PD/CA. Comparative wage scales from State of Michigan, *Annual Report of the Bureau of Labor and Industrial Statistics* (Lansing: W. S. George, 1884), pp. 82–87. Wage index, 1865–83, in Bureau of the Census, *Historical Statistics of the United States* (Washington: Government Printing Office, 1949), p. 66. For other cities, Wilbur R. Miller, Jr., *Cops and Bobbies: Police Authority in New York and London, 1830–1870* (Chicago: University of Chicago Press, 1977), pp. 31, 153–55; George A. Ketcham, "Municipal Police Reform: A Comparative Study of Law Enforcement in Cincinnati, Chicago, New Orleans, New York, and St. Louis, 1844–1877" (Ph.D. diss., University of Missouri, 1967), pp. 228–30.

19. Residences of professional police from Force Roster and Record Book "A" (1865–71), PD/CA. Names of the preprofessional policemen from lists of sheriff's deputies (criminal business only) in *Johnston's Detroit City Directory and Advertising Gazetteer of Michigan* (Detroit: H. Barns & Co., 1861), p. 25; *Charles F. Clark's Annual Directory of the Inhabitants, Incorporated Companies, Business Firms, etc. of the City of Detroit* (Detroit: Charles F. Clark, 1862), Appendix, pp. 3–4; *Charles F. Clark's Annual Directory of the Inhabitants, Incorporated Companies, Business Firms, etc., of the City of Detroit* (Detroit: Charles F. Clark, 1863), p. 284; list of special policemen appointed to help put down the rioting on the evening of March 6, 1863, in *Procs. C.C.* (1863), p. 248; and the list of policemen appointed to quell anticipated draft disturbances in early August 1863, in Special Police Record (1863), PD/CA. Except for this last list, which included them, residential addresses were obtained from the city directories, 1861–63.

20. *Free Press,* August 25, 1865; General and Special Orders, vol. 1 (1865–84): 5, PD/CA.

21. *Free Press,* May 15, 1865; *Rept. Police Comm.* (1866), pp. 4–5; *Rept. Police Comm.* (1874), p. 3; *Rept. Police Comm.* (1876), pp. 3–4, 12–14; *Rept. Police Comm.* (1881), pp. 14–15; Minutes of the Board of

Metropolitan Police Commissioners Meetings, vol. 3 (1883–90): 147, PD/CA.

22. *Rept. Police Comm.* (1870), pp. 25–26; *Rept. Police Comm.* (1876), pp. 12–14; *Rept. Police Comm.* (1878), pp. 3–4.

23. General and Special Orders, vol. 1 (1865–84): 45, 72, PD/CA.

24. *Manual for the Government of the Police,* pp. 1, 9.

25. *Ibid.,* p. 13; General and Special Orders, vol. 1 (1865–84): 4, 27, PD/CA.

26. Index of Suspicious Places and Record of Complaints (1865–68), pp. 1, 5, 9, 13, 17, 49, PD/CA.

27. *Rept. Police Comm.* (1878), p. 33; *Rept. Police Comm.* (1879), p. 33.

28. *Free Press,* October 21, 1879. For similar police concern about the new lodging houses in New York City, see Thomas Byrnes, "Nurseries of Crime," *North American Review* 149 (September 1889): 355–62.

29. *Free Press,* June 17, 27, July 1, 1865, June 12, July 20, August 4, 1866, January 27, June 28, July 16, November 22, 1867, March 26, September 25, October 8, 1868, February 2, 1870, July 19, 25, 1872; *Post,* June 27, 1867.

30. *Rept. House of Correction* (1870), pp. 11–12; *Acts of the Legislature of the State of Michigan, Passed at the Regular Session of 1869,* 3 vols. (Lansing: W. S. George, 1869), I: 264–69.

31. *News,* July 30, 1875. Arrest data from *Repts. Police Comm.* (1866–80). For police toleration of vice districts in other cities in the late nineteenth century, James F. Richardson, *The New York Police: Colonial Times to 1901* (New York: Oxford University Press, 1970), p. 186; Mark H. Haller, "Historical Roots of Police Behavior: Chicago, 1890–1925," *Law and Society Review* 10 (Winter 1976): 316.

32. Robert K. Bruce, *1877: Year of Violence* (Indianapolis: Bobbs-Merrill, 1959), pp. 20–22; Paul T. Ringenbach, *Tramps and Reformers, 1873–1916: The Discovery of Unemployment in New York* (Westport: Greenwood, 1973), pp. 3–29.

33. *Free Press,* December 13, 1873.

34. *Ibid.,* March 27, April 3, 1870, January 13, 1878; *Post,* July 23, 1877; *Procs. C.C.* (1869), pp. 327–29; *Procs. C.C.* (1870), pp. 123–24; *Mayor's Message* (1871), pp. 6–7; *Mayor's Message* (1879), pp. 35–36.

35. *Free Press,* January 7, 1876, December 20, 1878, January 25, 1879; *Post,* July 23, 1877; *Mayor's Message* (1876), pp. 17, 23.

36. *Free Press,* December 7, 1869, January 4, 1870, March 4, November 30, 1871, August 29–30, 1876, November 20, 1878; *Post,* January 4, 1873, December 4, 1875, *Post and Tribune,* December 6,

1878; *Mayor's Message* (1873), p. 10. The House of Correction was required by law to accept some prisoners from Michigan courts outside Detroit and Wayne County.

37. *Rept. Police Comm.* (1870), pp. 4–5, 25, 30; *Rept. Police Comm.* (1873), pp. 3–4; *Rept. Police Comm.* (1875), pp. 20–22; *Rept. Police Comm.* (1880), p. 26; *Mayor's Message* (1877), p. 13; *Post,* February 15, 1875.

38. *Manual for the Government of the Police,* p. 1; *Free Press,* July 20, November 25, 1865; *The Revised Ordinances of the City of Detroit* (Detroit: Free Press, 1871), pp. 175–76: *The Revised Ordinances of the City of Detroit* (Detroit: Union, 1878), p. 230; *The Revised Statutes of the State of Michigan* (Detroit: Bagg & Harmon, 1846), p. 182; *The Compiled Laws of the State of Michigan,* 2 vols. (Lansing: W. S. George, 1872), 1:644–45.

39. *Free Press,* January 4, December 17, 1870, March 4, 1871, February 5, 1874, August 29–30, 1876, June 14, November 20, 1878; *Post,* January 4, 1873, December 4, 1875; General and Special Orders, vol. 1 (1865–84): 30, PD/CA.

40. For the increase in public order arrests by new professional forces elsewhere, Allan E. Levett, "Centralization of City Police in Nineteenth-Century United States" (Ph.D. diss., University of Michigan, 1974), pp. 54–55.

41. Preprofessional data from Police Court arraignments, reported in *Free Press,* January 6, April 15, July 4, October 8, 1863, January 7, April 4, July 6, October 16, 1864. Police Court statistics may slightly understate actual public order arrest totals since, until the organization of the professional police, misdemeanor offenders were sometimes brought before justices of the peace.

42. Ibid., May 12, 1877.

43. Ibid., July 24, 1877. Also, August 11, 1867, July 26, 29, 1877; *Post,* July 24–August 2, 1877.

44. *Free Press,* July 24, 1868, June 2, 9, 1874; *Post,* June 1–2, 1874.

45. *Free Press,* July 24–27, 1877.

46. General and Special Orders, vol. 1 (1865–84): 79, PD/CA; General Arrest Ledger, vol. 6 (1876–78), July 24–26, 1877, PD/CA; *Free Press,* July 27, 1877. For tough police action against tramps in Buffalo during the depression of the 1890s, see Sidney L. Harring, "Class Conflict and the Suppression of Tramps in Buffalo, 1892–1894," *Law and Society Review* 11 (Summer 1977): 873–911.

47. The first sample (N=868) began April 1, 1869, and ended March 31, 1871. Every eighth name was recorded, after a random start of three. The second sample (N=918) began February 1, 1879, and ended January 31, 1881. Every ninth name was recorded, after a

random start of seven. The monthly dates correspond to those used by the police department in compiling aggregate data for the annual report. Samples were drawn from General Arrest Ledger, vol. 3 (1869–71), vol. 7 (1878–80), vol. 8 (1880–81), PD/CA.

48. Robert V. Percival, using similar police arrest data, found that more than a quarter of all arrested persons in Oakland, California, from 1872 to 1910 were from out of town. Robert V. Percival, "Municipal Justice in the Melting Pot: Arrest and Prosecution in Oakland, 1872–1910" (Paper presented at the Conference on Historical Perspectives on American Criminal Justice, Omaha, Nebraska, April 23, 1976), p. 30.

49. Arthur Stinchcombe, "Institutions of Privacy in the Determination of Police Administrative Practice," *American Journal of Sociology* 69 (September 1963): 157. Also, James Q. Wilson, *Varieties of Police Behavior: The Management of Law and Order in Eight Communities* (Cambridge: Harvard University Press, 1968), pp. 118–20.

50. *People* v. *Mahoney* (1865), 13 Michigan 481; William B. Lord and David W. Brown, eds., *The Debates and Proceedings of the Constitutional Convention of the State of Michigan,* 2 vols. (Lansing: John A. Kerr, 1867), 2: 331–54; *Free Press,* June 10, 1865, July 30, 1867, January 14, February 28, 1877; *Procs. C.C.* (1877), p. 594; *Mayor's Message* (1874), pp. 4–5; *Mayor's Message* (1878), p. 3.

51. *Free Press,* July 30, 1867, February 25, 1868, February 28, 1877; *Procs. C.C.* (1868), pp. 367–69; *Rept. Police Comm.* (1866), p. 4.

52. *Free Press,* November 29, 1865. Also, December 14, 1865, June 2, 1867; *Post,* April 24, 1866, January 23, 1875. For contemporary attitudes about dangerous subcultures and policing, William A. Westley, *Violence and the Police: A Sociological Study of Law, Custom, and Morality* (Cambridge: MIT Press, 1970), p. 107; Egon Bittner, "The Police on Skid Row: A Study in Peace Keeping," *American Sociological Review* 32 (October 1967): 704–7.

53. General and Special Orders, vol. 1 (1865–84): 10, PD/CA; *Free Press,* July 27, 1866, January 28, 1873, June 17, 1877; *Post,* July 27, 1866, February 28, 1873, July 29, 1874; Miller, *Cops and Bobbies,* pp. 140–48. Data on weapons-carrying from the arrest samples of 1869–71 and 1879–81. Police blotters recorded all property found on the person arrested.

54. *Manual of the Metropolitan Police Force of the City of Detroit* (Detroit: Tribune, 1872), pp. 87–90; General and Special Orders, vol. 1 (1865–84): 24–47, PD/CA; *Free Press,* October 1, 1874; *Rept. Police Comm.* (1868), p. 24. Trials of patrolmen reported in Minutes of the Board of Metropolitan Police Commissioners Meetings, vol. 1 (1865–75), vol. 2 (1875–83), vol. 3 (1883–90), PD/CA.

55. Minutes of the Board of Metropolitan Police Commissioners Meetings, vol. 2 (1875–83): 198–205, PD/CA.

56. Richard V. Ericson, "Police Bureaucracy and Decision-Making: The Function of Discretion in Maintaining the Police System," in Jack Goldsmith and Sharon S. Goldsmith, eds., *The Police Community: Dimensions of an Occupational Subculture* (Pacific Palisades: Palisades, 1974), pp. 93–94; Susan O. White, "A Perspective on Police Professionalization," in ibid., pp. 39–62.

57. Miller, *Cops and Bobbies,* p. 155. Also, Arthur Niederhoffer, *Behind the Shield: The Police in Urban Society* (Garden City: Doubleday, 1967), pp. 193–94.

FIVE: THE RETURN TO ORDER

1. *Free Press,* July 16, 1867, September 17–18, 1869, January 5, 1875, October 31, 1876.

2. Ibid., May 1, 1872, March 11, July 11, 1873, December 8, 1874.

3. Ibid., July 27, 1877.

4. Ibid., August 6, September 13, November 25, 1865, October 12, 1869.

5. James Q. Wilson, *Varieties of Police Behavior: The Management of Law and Order in Eight Communities* (Cambridge: Harvard University Press, 1968), pp. 126–28; Egon Bittner, "The Police on Skid Row: A Study of Peace Keeping," *American Sociological Review* 32 (October 1967): 706–7; Albert B. Wolfe, *The Lodging House Problem in Boston* (Boston: Houghton, Mifflin, 1906), p. 137.

6. *Post and Tribune,* February 16, 1880.

7. *Free Press,* July 2, 1865.

8. Ibid., July 2, 1865, July 31, 1867, January 13, 1876, May 15, 1877; *Rept. Police Comm.* (1876), pp. 3–4.

9. The great increase in the number of incidents reported compared with 1854 and 1864 is a reflection not only of the growth of the city's population but also of more thorough reporting by the *Free Press* (no item seemed too trivial—a pair of trousers stolen from a clothesline, for example) and the completeness of the police information systems on which it depended. Criminal residential patterns in the map are based on 1879–81 sample (see Table IV–5).

10. Jane Jacobs, *The Death and Life of Great American Cities* (New York: Random House, 1961), pp. 29–54.

11. *Free Press,* January 17, 1869.

12. For mid-twentieth-century patterns, Calvin F. Schmid, "Urban Crime Areas: Part II," *American Sociological Review* 25 (October

1960): 678; Keith D. Harries, *The Geography of Crime and Justice* (New York: McGraw-Hill, 1974), p. 61; Sarah L. Boggs, "Urban Crime Patterns," in Daniel Glazer, ed., *Crime in the City* (New York: Harper, 1970), pp. 116–18.

13. Charles Tilly, "Collective Violence in European Perspective," in Hugh D. Graham and Ted R. Gurr, eds., *Violence in America: Historical and Comparative Perspectives*, 2 vols. (Washington: Government Printing Office, 1969), 1:24. For overviews of American urban disorder, Richard M. Brown, *Strain of Violence: Historical Studies of American Violence and Vigilantism* (New York: Oxford University Press, 1975), ch. 1; Richard C. Wade, "Violence in the Cities: A Historical View," in Charles V. Daly, ed., *Urban Violence* (Chicago: University of Chicago Press, 1969), pp. 7–26.

14. Edith Abbott, "The Civil War and the Crime Wave of 1865–1870," *Social Service Review* 1 (June 1927): 212–34; Edwin Powell, "Crime as a Function of Anomie," *Journal of Criminal Law, Criminology, and Police Science* 57 (June 1966): 161–71; Theodore N. Ferdinand, "The Criminal Patterns of Boston Since 1849," *American Journal of Sociology* 73 (July 1967): 84–99, and "Politics, the Police, and Arresting Policies in Salem, Massachusetts, Since the Civil War," *Social Problems* 19 (Spring 1972): 572–88; Eric H. Monkkonen, *The Dangerous Class: Crime and Poverty in Columbus, Ohio, 1860–1885* (Cambridge: Harvard University Press, 1975), ch. 3; Robert V. Percival, "Municipal Justice in the Melting Pot: Arrest and Prosecution in Oakland, 1872–1910" (Paper presented at the Conference on Historical Perspectives on American Criminal Justice, Omaha, Nebraska, April 23, 1976). A recent investigation of Pittsburgh in the late nineteenth century is interesting for its analysis of crime as a function of class conflict, but the period studied is a bit brief to make meaningful comparisons with the above studies. As it was, there was a slight rise in property crime and an equally slight decline in personal crime in Pittsburgh between 1870 and 1890. See James F. Caye, "Crime and Violence in the Heterogeneous Urban Community: Pittsburgh, 1870–1889" (Ph.D. diss., University of Pittsburgh, 1977), pp. 70, 74.

15. Adrian Cook, *The Armies of the Street: The New York City Draft Riots of 1863* (Lexington: University of Kentucky Press, 1974), pp. 208–9. Also, Sam Bass Warner, Jr., *The Private City: Philadelphia in Three Periods of its Growth* (Philadelphia: University of Pennsylvania Press, 1968), p. 156.

16. Monkkonen, *Dangerous Class*, pp. 104–5; Ferdinand, "Criminal Patterns of Boston," pp. 97–99.

17. Roger Lane, "Urbanization and Criminal Violence in the Nineteenth Century: Massachusetts as a Test Case," in Graham and

Gurr, eds., *Violence in America*, 2: 359–70; Warner, *Private City*, pp. 161–69; Monkkonen, *Dangerous Class*, pp. 32–33; Michael Feldberg, *The Philadelphia Riots of 1844: A Study of Ethnic Conflict* (Westport, Conn.: Greenwood, 1975), pp. 178–79.

18. Carl Wittke, *The Irish in America* (Baton Rouge: Louisiana State University Press, 1956), pp. 125–34.

19. Alan Booth, Susan Welch, and David R. Johnson, "Crowding and Urban Crime Rates," *Urban Affairs Quarterly* 11 (March 1976): 291–308.

20. Gerald Suttles, "Deviant Behavior as an Unanticipated Consequence of Public Housing," in Glazer, *Crime in the City*, pp. 162–76; Oscar Newman, *Defensible Space: Crime Prevention Through Urban Design* (New York: Macmillan, 1973).

21. Kathleen Neils Conzen makes this point nicely in *Immigrant Milwaukee, 1836–1860: Accommodation and Community in a Frontier City* (Cambridge: Harvard University Press, 1976), pp. 127–31.

22. Michael Feldberg, "The Crowd in Philadelphia History: A Comparative Perspective," *Labor History* 5 (Summer 1974): 329–30.

A NOTE ON THE DETROIT SOURCES

The chapter notes can serve adequately as a bibliography for the interested reader. But since so much of this study rests on evidence from Detroit archival sources cited but not often described in the text or the notes, a few words about the most important of these are appropriate.

Manuscripts. The Burton Historical Collection at the Detroit Public Library has an abundance of manuscript material on Detroit dating from the nineteenth century. It received some of this material in its capacity as the official city archives, including the records of the police department. I found these records a bit difficult to work with at first because someone had erred in cataloguing many of them, confusing police board minutes with court dockets in one instance, for example. I corrected these errors where I found them, and the staff at the Burton Collection has on file my corrected listing of the police department records. Once past this hurdle, I discovered these holdings to be a superb collection, all the more so in the light of the difficulties historians have had in locating good police records for nineteenth-century cities. On this problem, one might refer to the exchange between Harvey J. Graff and Eric Monkkonen in *Journal of Interdisciplinary History* 7 (Winter 1977): 477–91; 9 (Winter 1979): 451–71.

The records of the Metropolitan Police Department organized in 1865 comprise most of the nineteenth-century manuscript material on the police in the city archives. There were several items I used extensively. The Minutes of the Board of Metropolitan Police Commissioners Meetings, in five volumes

(1865–1905), contain much information on routine matters of administration, but they also include the specifics—name of officer, charge, testimony, verdict—on every police disciplinary case that came before the commissioners. The General and Special Orders, in ten volumes (1865–1915), are a record of the commands that went down the ranks from the superintendent or the commissioners and include everything from instructions on the proper wearing of the uniform to directives on tramp arrests and the carrying of firearms. Force Roster and Record Book "A" (1865–71) contains the names of all the men appointed to the force in the first five and a half years of the department, along with each man's age, marital status, number of children, place of birth (U.S. state, foreign country), occupation, and local address—all of these, of course, at the time of his appointment to the force. Books "B" and "C" are apparently lost, but the Burton Collection has Books "D" and "E" covering the years 1889–1909. Finally, I made considerable use of the General Arrest Register, which runs to forty volumes (1865–1912). This was the official police blotter and describes every arrest made by the department from the first day patrolmen took the streets. Information recorded includes date of arrest; station reporting arrest; arrestee's name, age, occupation, marital status, race, place of birth (U.S. state, foreign country), and effects; offense for which arrest made; arresting officer; and final disposition of the case, although until vol. 10 (1883–84) this was not always recorded if the case went beyond the Police Court. The arrestee's place of residence (local street address, Michigan town, city, etc. outside Detroit, U.S. state if other than Michigan) was recorded beginning with vol. 7 (1878–80).

Published Municipal Records. The Burton Collection has a complete run of the published proceedings of the Common Council, 1830–80. The first two volumes cover the years 1824–43 and 1844–52. Beginning in 1853, the proceedings were published annually by the city. These volumes contain more than just motions, resolutions, ordinances, and roll call votes. They also include committee reports, petitions, and communications from other city officials.

Of the annual reports by various city boards, departments, and officials, I found two most useful. The Board of Water Commissioners was established in 1853 and its first annual report was published that year. The Burton Collection has many, but not all, of these annual reports for the period through 1880. They provide some interesting information about the city that I found helpful in reconstructing spatial patterns. For example, each volume includes a ward-by-ward enumeration of various types of buildings, such as boarding houses, stores, factories, saloons, and offices. The Board of Metropolitan Police Commissioners published its first annual report in 1866. The Burton Collection has all of these reports through 1880 except that of 1867. They contain a wealth of data about the administration and operation of the police department. The most important data were total number of arrests by offense; total number of arrestees by occupation, sex, race, place of birth (U.S., foreign country), age group, and marital status (the last two pieces of information unavailable in the first report); total number of overnight lodgers by sex and place of birth (U.S., non–U.S.); and total number of policemen and their distribution by station.

All dates in parentheses accompanying the abbreviated citation of annual city documents in the notes are dates of publication. For the first two volumes of the proceedings of the Common Council, I included the years covered in each volume. Their dates of publication are unclear.

Newspapers. Evidence from the newspapers was the foundation on which much of this study rests, despite their partisan political stances that sometimes interfered with objective reporting and despite the spotty reporting of local news until the late 1840s. I relied mainly on three weekly papers for the 1830s: the *Detroit Courier* (1831–35), the *Detroit Journal and Michigan Advertiser* (1830–35), and the *Detroit Journal and Courier* (1835–39). I also used the semi-weekly *Detroit Journal and Advertiser* (1834–35). For the succeeding years I turned principally to the *Detroit Free Press,* the city's major Democratic paper, founded in 1831, and published daily after 1835. It is a valuable source not only because of its good and consistent coverage of local news, but also because it often printed information unavailable in any other form (for example, police court data before 1865). I supplemented the *Free Press* in the 1840–70 period with two important Whig-Republican dailies: the *Detroit Daily Advertiser* (1836–62) and the *Detroit Advertiser and Tribune* (1862–70); and in the period after 1870 with the *Detroit Daily Post,* also a Republican paper, which began publication in 1866. The *Post* became the *Detroit Post and Tribune* in 1877.

Directories. As historians of the nineteenth-century city have come to find out, city directories can be invaluable research tools, not simply for their listings of residents, but also for the data about the city they often presented in their introductions and appendices. Detroit's were no exception. The Burton Collection has all the directories published in the city between 1830 and 1880. Until 1850, there were but a few of them—in 1837, 1845, and 1846. After 1850 they appeared more frequently, and by the 1860s they were published annually.

Clarence M. Burton, founder of the Burton Collection, reconstructed the 1837 directory by streets and alleys. This is available in bound typescript at the Burton Collection and proved helpful to me in determining Detroit's early spatial arrangements. The compiler of the 1853 directory included a census he took of the city (Table I–1), which enumerated the population by ward according to religion and national origin— e.g. French Catholics, German Protestants, American Methodists. It is unclear how he determined national origin. Many of those he describes as French, for instance, were obviously Canadians by birth. For the three principal groups—native-born, German, Irish—I assumed this census to be reasonably accurate. The directories of 1862, 1863, 1865, 1875, and 1880 contain regular business directories, as distinct from the indexes to advertisers that generally were included. I used these business directories to locate saloons, billiard halls, and boarding houses, recognizing all the while that the directories probably did not include many of the smaller or least respectable of these places. The number of saloons and boarding houses listed in the directories were never as great as those reported in the annual statements of the Board of Water Commissioners.

The list of boarding houses in the 1875 directory is obviously more incomplete than usual, and so I used instead the 1880 directory to plot them with saloons, billiard halls, and vice districts (Map IV–3). The private "carriage directory" of Detroit published by B. E. Fanning in 1876 and available at the Burton Collection was a valuable find. It lists in alphabetical order the streets on which Detroit's "first class people" resided, and includes under each street the house numbers and names of these fashionable residents.

Maps. The preeminent cartographer of nineteenth-century Detroit was Silas Farmer (1839–1902), and I used his maps whenever possible. The Burton Collection has many of Farmer's maps, as well as a variety of others. Although it is not reproduced in this study, Farmer's *Guide Map of Detroit* published in 1872 was indispensable, for it was one of the few maps of the city that included block-by-block street numbers. I used this map as the base for all of my plottings. The superlative "bird's-eye" map of Detroit in chapter two (Map II–1) is dated 1849 in the Burton Collection, but Silas Farmer, who ought to have known, says in his *History of Detroit and Michigan, or The Metropolis Illustrated* (Detroit: Silas Farmer, 1884), p. 374, that it was done in 1853 by Henry Hart.

A final note on population statistics and the per thousand capita crime rates in Tables III–1 and V–1: Detroit population figures are available for the federal census years (1850, 1860, 1870, 1880), the state census years (1854, 1864, 1874, 1884), and years in which local censuses of one kind or another were taken (1845, 1853, 1868). For all other years I computed the total population by averaging out the population gain from one census to the next.

INDEX